How to Read a
COUNTRY
HOUSE

How to Read a
COUNTRY
HOUSE

JEREMY MUSSON

IN ASSOCIATION WITH
COUNTRY LIFE

EBURY PRESS
LONDON

DEDICATED TO ELIZABETH, ONE OF LIFE'S GREAT ENTHUSIASTS

2 3 4 5 6 7 8 9 10

First published in Great Britain in 2005

The *How to Read* series is based on an original idea by Richard Taylor.

First published by Ebury Press
Random House, 20 Vauxhall Bridge Road, London SW1V 2SA
Random House Australia (Pty) Limited
20 Alfred Street, Milsons Point, Sydney, New South Wales 2061, Australia
Random House New Zealand Limited
18 Poland Road, Glenfield, Auckland 10, New Zealand
Random House South Africa (Pty) Limited
Endulini, 5A Jubilee Road, Parktown 2193, South Africa

The Random House Group Limited Reg. No. 954009
www.randomhouse.co.uk

A CIP catalogue record for this book is available from the British Library.

Editor: Belinda Wilkinson
Series editor: Richard Taylor
Designer: David Fordham
Line drawings by Rodney Paull

ISBN 0 0919 0076 X
ISBN 9780091900762 (from January 2007)

Papers used by Ebury Press are natural, recyclable products
made from wood grown in sustainable forests.

Printed and bound in Singapore by Tien Wah Press.

PAGE 1: *An early 18th-century chimneypiece at Frampton Court in Gloucestershire.*
PAGE 2: *Designed around a Tudor core, Owlpen Manor, Gloucestershire, has a Jacobean wing to the left and 18th-century windows to the right.*
PAGE 3: *A typically mellow country house, Womersley Hall, Yorkshire, with its later Georgian front.*
PAGE 5: *Robert Adam's glorious sculpture gallery at Newby Hall, Yorkshire.*

CONTENTS

READING A COUNTRY HOUSE

Why Read a Country House?

LIKE THE ENGLISH parish church, the English country house might seem a deceptively familiar concept, but it encompasses a long history with diverse strands. Even if one can agree on a broad definition of a country house as, perhaps, the major residence of a landowner or the centre of a country estate, it is still a big subject with many different aspects.

The history of the English country house spans at least eight centuries, ranging from the castles and manors of the twelfth century (and earlier) to the ornate and handsome country houses of the Tudor and Jacobean eras, through the stately Classical houses of the late seventeenth and

LEFT: *Perhaps the most romantic image of an English country house, Haddon Hall in Derbyshire has been a residence of the Manners family since 1563. Built around a large courtyard, Haddon was extended over several different periods, particularly during the 15th and early 16th centuries, and carefully restored in the 1920s.*

RIGHT: *The breathtaking Elizabethan mansion Hardwick Hall, Derbyshire, was built in the 1590s for the famous Bess of Hardwick, Countess of Shrewsbury. The design of its main rooms, arranged in storeys, and its fashionable expanse of great and expensive windows led to the local quip, 'Hardwick Hall, More Glass than Wall'.*

eighteenth centuries to the mansions, great and small, in the varied styles of the late eighteenth and nineteenth centuries. Last but not least, the story of the country house encompasses the plush retreats of the Edwardian millionaires right up to the post-modern country retreats of the late twentieth century and today.

But however long and wide-ranging its history, one facet of the country house has remained constant, and that is display. Country houses have always been about display. They were built to be looked at, not just to be lived in. With this in mind, *How to Read a Country House* explores the visible evidence encountered in the various houses, and aims to 'read', or explain, the visual clues.

How to Read a Country House is not intended as a literary or cultural history of country houses, but rather as a guide to interpreting and understanding the different aspects of a house that are likely to be encountered on a visit. I have adopted the approach that I use when writing articles for *Country Life* magazine. First I describe what can actually be seen, then I wonder what more could be gleaned by studying any literature or documents about the house.

It is hoped that this guidebook will serve as a handy companion to the many country house enthusiasts who want to discover more about what they see as they wander around the exterior and interior of a house. *How to Read a Country House* describes the notable features of country houses, including the key period details of such vital elements as windows and doorways, as well as the symbolism used in decoration. Symbolism typically emerges in the house's heraldry, signifying the prestige and power of the family, and in Classical allusion. I have chosen all the photographs from *Country Life*'s unrivalled picture library.

The final section offers a suggested reading list for anyone wishing to go beyond this introductory survey based principally on the immediate visual evidence. Also provided at the end is a selection of 200 country houses open to the public, as well as a selection of significant houses representing the design of each major period, which aims to highlight useful general characteristics.

When considering the histories of country houses, it helps to be realistic about the motives behind the building. The commonest ambition in founding a house was not just to impress onlookers but to build a landed dynasty. To get a real sense of the purpose of the country house

one needs to imagine the desire to found a 'line' and to maintain it. Ambitious men, and occasionally women, have through the centuries fiercely sought political power and influence for themselves, their family and future generations. Landed estates were a ticket into the ruling class, through politics and public office – and a good investment too.

The ambition for lasting status taken to extremes explains some of the 'folies de grandeur', from the Tudor age to the twentieth century, including some of our finest mansions, such as Hardwick Hall in Derbyshire and Burghley House in Lincolnshire. Such grand mansions were not built for one individual but rather for a great family; they were founded and embellished as part of a conscious mission to establish a 'line' with all the prestige and access to privilege that was bound up with the perceived security and status of pedigree and landowning. Dynastic ambition rides like a fierce wave through eight centuries, only really declining in intensity during the twentieth.

To anyone remotely interested in country houses, the history of the family plays a vital part in the story of the house itself. Alongside the often compelling sagas of the founder father, there are also the stories of those who came after the founding spirit, sometimes secure and happy in their inheritance, sometimes less so. Succeeding generations had their own ambitions to fulfil, alliances

and dynastic marriages to make, duties and services to perform, privilege and prestige to enjoy; they experienced their own hopes and fears, successes and failures, heroics and acts of folly.

Every country house has a wider cast of characters, too, beyond the family. Alongside the histories of the family's varied members – its bold soldiers, courtiers or lucky inheritors – are the stories of the designer of the house, the professional mason or gentleman amateur architect (of the seventeenth and early eighteenth centuries), the professional architect (of the nineteenth and twentieth centuries), and the skilled and unskilled craftsmen, artists, silversmiths and furniture makers, who built, decorated and furnished country houses. There are also the stories of the household staff who ran the stately machine, making possible the lifestyle and status enjoyed in a country house.

It should also be stressed that the architecture, setting and contents of the most enjoyable country houses are rarely brought together in a single generation, but laid up over the centuries by different generations who, even in their earnest desire to continue the efforts of their forebears, always stamp their mark on a house.

COUNTRY HOUSES: THE POWER OF THE PAST

ONE OF THE joys of country house visiting in England is that so much has, against the odds, survived, whereas in other European countries so much has been dispersed by major wars or by laws of inheritance that are designed to share property equally between heirs. By contrast, Britain's tough tradition of primogeniture means that the bulk of an estate passes to the eldest son.

To appreciate the character of such a house, it might help to recall the words of the artist Charles Ryder in Evelyn Waugh's *Brideshead Revisited* (1945):

> *More even than the work of great architects, I loved buildings that grew silently with the centuries, catching and keeping the best of each generation, while time curbed the artist's pride and the Philistine's vulgarity, and repaired the clumsiness of the dull workman.*

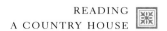

ABOVE: *The three main Classical orders are* (LEFT TO RIGHT) *Doric,
Ionic (here flanking the lower doorway) and Corinthian. They each have
their own distinctive details, especially the capital, capping the column.*

For me, a good example of a house that has captured 'the best of each generation' is Stonor Park
in Oxfordshire. Seat of the Lord Camoys, Stonor has been in the hands of the Stonor family for
eight centuries. It presents a smiling sixteenth-century red-brick elevation with Georgian sashes,
the last of many layers of earlier houses. Think too of Berkeley Castle in Gloucestershire, which
has been in the same family's possession since the twelfth century. Berkeley possesses elements
of addition and embellishment over many centuries that nonetheless come together in a
satisfying and mature whole. The Berkeleys, who are still resident, can trace their lineage back to
an aristocratic Anglo-Saxon supporter of the Norman king William the Conqueror.

Among those responsible for the care and restoration of country houses, there has often been
a temptation to return to what might be one house's notional golden age, as if there was one
moment when all the best qualities were fully expressed, and worthy of preserving for future
generations. But in my view focusing on just one period means one misses out on all the glorious
oddities, along with the human story of the house.

It is interesting to think how long the tradition of trying to hold on to or recapture the past has
influenced English taste. William Morris, the nineteenth-century designer, poet and social

RIGHT: *A handsome Cotswold manor house, Kelmscott Manor in Oxfordshire became the country retreat of the designer William Morris during the late 19th century. Morris did much to increase people's awareness of the beauty of older buildings, influencing Arts and Crafts thinking, and also founding the Society for the Protection of Ancient Buildings.*

reformer, and founder of the Society for the Protection of Ancient Buildings, helped open people's eyes to the beauty of the layers of ages; and to see that modest alterations and honest repairs were often the genuine and most unselfconscious expressions of an age.

His own weekend retreat was the delectable Cotswold stone Kelmscott Manor in Oxfordshire, which represented to him a kind of ideal. Morris wrote in *News From Nowhere* (1890) that Kelmscott 'had grown up out of the soil and the lives of them that lived on it'.

Morris and the art critic Ruskin are often seen as having set in train a way of thinking about the past that persists today and that has become fundamental to British culture. Their ideas were the seed for the spirit of legislation that sought and still seeks to preserve the best architectural remains of the past; and that has informed the role of the National Trust, English Heritage and other bodies, such as the Georgian Group and the Victorian Society.

Yet the idea of preserving our past has been around for a while. One of my personal historical heroes, the great playwright-turned-architect John Vanbrugh, who designed Castle Howard in Yorkshire and Blenheim in Oxfordshire, wrote to the Duchess of Marlborough on 11 June 1709 pleading to be allowed to retain the ruin of the old royal manor of Woodstock:

> *There is no one thing which the most Polite part of Mankind have more universally agreed in – that the Vallue they have ever set upon the Remains of distant Times, Not amongst the severall kinds of those Antiquitys, are there any so well regarded as those of Buildings. Some for their Magnificence, or Curious Workmanship; And others; as they move more lively and pleasing Reflections (than History without their aid can do) on the persons who have Inhabited them; on the Remarkable things which have been translated in them, of the extraordinary occasions of erecting Them.*

Yet in an era before major heritage bodies existed to save important buildings, family fortunes rose and fell and sometimes their houses fell with them. This happened at an alarming rate in

the mid-twentieth century. James Lees-Milne, who did so much to negotiate the transfer of historic country houses to the National Trust during and immediately after World War II, famously wrote in 1974, 'the English country house is as archaic as the osprey'.

Actually both the osprey and the English country house have fared better than expected in the last fifty years. The work of the Liberal politician Lord Lothian and of Lees-Milne himself in the 1940s, reinforced by the Gowers report on the cultural importance of country houses (commissioned by Clement Attlee's Labour government), began the very slow turning of the tide.

The National Trust's commitment, and the efforts of many private owners and organizations such as the Historic Houses Association, many local authorities and thousands of volunteers and enthusiasts have helped to preserve, record and reveal the importance of the country house in our shared culture. Country houses in England have been admired across the western world, particularly in the eighteenth and nineteenth centuries, and thus form part of the identity of our island. They have also, as Vanbrugh remarked, provided the backdrops for our national history.

The country house is a place where politics, religion, literature, economics, art, craftsmanship, labour and trades have all left their mark. In the big spaces of country houses, the authentic flavour of the past has somehow managed to survive, in striking comparison to the quick evaporation of the past in the smaller houses in which most of us live.

Certainly country houses cannot be understood in complete isolation, and anyone interested in architectural history needs to examine the country house alongside many other things – parish churches, the ruins of monasteries, homes in towns and villages, and the great industrial sites of the eighteenth and nineteenth centuries, such as the docks, canals and railways.

Viewing a house in its local and historical context is, after all, the way country houses have been presented in the magisterial series, *The Buildings of England* (1951–74), edited and originally largely written by Nikolaus Pevsner. The series, which provides a county-by-county architectural guide, has been constantly updated. The original guide has now been extended to *The Buildings of Wales* (1979–2005) and *The Buildings of Scotland* (1992–2000); a *Buildings of Ireland* is in progress.

But arguably other histories, such as those of industry and commerce, must also be read alongside country houses. These houses, indeed, were often created by industry and commerce (sometimes from unpalatably exploitative fields, such as slavery or armaments). Country houses are part of the warp and weft of our history, exhibiting much of the best art and design of the British Isles; they are monuments to great hopes, and homes to quite complex communities (even today), as well as to individuals. Open to the public in great number in this country, they are waiting to be visited and enjoyed.

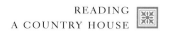

LEFT: *Little Moreton Hall, Cheshire, a magnificent timber-framed manor house, built in two phases during the 16th century. Before the 17th century timber was a principal building material for country house construction outside the good stone quarrying areas. After the early 17th century brick manufacture and improved transport meant that no major houses were built of timber frame.*

Looking over the Centuries

B Y WAY OF introduction to the discussion of significant details and symbols that follows, I would like briefly to sketch out an overview of the evolution of the English country house. Where do we begin? In terms of surviving examples, it is probably reasonable to begin in the twelfth century following the Norman Conquest of 1066, when the Duke of Normandy became William I of England and redistributed much of the landholding to his followers and supporters from Normandy.

I say 'landholding', because at that date concepts of ownership were different from now, and land was held directly or indirectly from the crown, in return for services, military or other. Landholding was the basis of the feudal system that dominated English affairs for centuries, and continues to be felt in certain legal or manorial rights, such as holding a fair, up to the present day.

The newly built Norman castles constructed in stone around the country for the king or his tenants-in-chief were military buildings and undoubtedly also symbols of William's great conquest. But they were always designed to incorporate some degree of dwelling or residence, even if essentially temporary in character. The mighty Norman edifice of Rochester Castle in Kent, for instance, built for the bishops of Rochester in 1127, had no fewer than three sets of grand residential apartments.

There were also manor house complexes in the Norman tradition, fragments of which still survive today, notably at late twelfth-century The Manor House, Boothby Pagnell in Lincolnshire, and The Manor, Hemingford Grey in Cambridgeshire. Both these two-storey stone buildings, with their distinctive round-headed windows and doors, were originally constructed as one single room on the first floor, with a single vaulted space beneath for storage.

Such manor houses were once believed to be examples of a first-floor hall type, but are now thought more likely to have been sturdily built chamber blocks that included the private apartment of the lord of the manor and his family. They were almost certainly accompanied by a separate timber-built hall and kitchen block.

LEFT: *A stone-built room, part of the surviving late 12th-century chamber block at The Manor, Hemingford Grey, Cambridgeshire. Originally built as a single, large, first-floor room, it would probably have been accompanied by a timber-framed hall. The Manor is thought to be one of the oldest continuously occupied houses in England.*

The hall is part of a much longer tradition, a centre for a community as much as a room; the mede-hall referred to in the Anglo-Saxon poem *Beowulf* still conjures up the image of a sanctuary for warriors, designed for feasting and storytelling. The hall (or great hall, as it became known, in the sense of being 'big') is the essential ingredient of a dwelling of status from the 1100s to the early 1600s, be it great castle, bishop's palace or humble manor.

By the thirteenth century, the chamber block was connected to one end of the hall, the kitchens to the other, creating a formula that was shared in a number of variations by most manor houses until the sixteenth century. If we were to look at manor houses ranging in date from the late thirteenth to the late fifteenth centuries, it would become clear how the key elements remained loosely consistent over the centuries. Typical examples might be Stokesay Castle in

RIGHT: *Stokesay Castle, Shropshire provides a well-preserved example of a 13th-century manor-house complex, with its tall windows indicating the presence of the great hall at its centre. The whole structure would originally have been enclosed by a wall and gatehouse.*

RIGHT: *Lacock Abbey, Wiltshire, one of the many gentry houses contrived from a former monastic establishment after the dissolution of the monasteries from 1536 to 1540. The cloister is immediately recognisable here.*

Shropshire, *c.* 1290s, Cothay Manor in Somerset, *c.* 1380s, and Great Chalfield Manor in Wiltshire, *c.* 1460s.

The great hall was, in essence, a large rectangular room open to the height of the pitched roof. In scale, it often appears more like a covered courtyard than a room. But it was always intended to be capacious and capable of different tasks. It was the hub of life at the manor, where the lord, his family and immediate household sat; it was also the administrative centre of local life, and of the district over which the lord of the manor held sway.

It was in the hall that courts and major gatherings were held and where, at first, the family and household ate together, communally, but seated according to a strict hierarchy. The lord and his family sat at one end, on a table raised on a dais. The private first-floor chamber was placed conveniently at that end.

The kitchen was usually at the other end of the great hall, and food seems to have been brought in with some ceremony. The entrance to the kitchen was placed between two smaller rooms, one being the pantry, for the preparation of bread (after the French *pain*); the other being the buttery, for the preparation of beer, and also the butler's domain (after the French *bouteilleur* for bottle-bearer). The entrance to the hall was also usually found at this end, furthest from the lord's end, and it led into a passageway created by means of a screen, designed to cut down on draughts.

By the fourteenth century, most great halls were crowned with a glorious timber ceiling supporting a high roof. The nature of ritual dining with the household changed so that by the late thirteenth and early fourteenth century the lord and his family would usually dine privately in a great chamber, leaving his steward to dine at the dais end, presiding over the rest of the household. By the fifteenth century it was common to provide an everyday family dining parlour below the great chamber, as can be seen at Haddon Hall in Derbyshire.

The great hall and related chambers were, of course, usually the nucleus of a much larger structure, with lodgings for retainers in wings around a courtyard, as in the well-preserved example at Sudeley Castle in Gloucestershire. This courtyard plan is also exemplified by the older colleges of the universities of Oxford and Cambridge, such as Oxford's New College.

Castles to power houses

Castles of the fourteenth and fifteenth centuries, such as Bodiam in Sussex, Herstmonceux in Sussex and Tattershall in Lincolnshire, seem, in every visible way, to be fortified, yet also seem to be great houses, designed in the tradition of earlier medieval castles, with effective use of geometry and symmetry in the disposition of the towers and gatehouse.

A royal licence was required (between the thirteenth and seventeenth centuries) to crenellate a residence, by which a lord paid for the royal recognition of his right to turn his home into a castle, permission for which was sought for reasons of status as well as defence.

Henry VIII's palaces were great houses built around large courtyards, with fanciful skylines, created by pinnacles and highly decorated chimneys, recalling the fluttering pennants of a knightly tournament. A fine example is the Tudor palace, Hampton Court, initiated by Cardinal Wolsey but completed by Henry VIII.

Tudor period gatehouses were regarded as good vehicles for dramatic architectural statement, as seen at Layer Marney in Essex. By the 1500s, Classical details, such as Greco-Roman columns and miniature temples, appeared in English architecture, inspired by the Renaissance, a revival of Classical culture that started in Italy in the fifteenth century, spreading to Northern Europe during the sixteenth century. The concurrent development of printing ensured a wide circulation of Classically inspired images, which could be used as source material.

Henry VIII's two great swipes at the long-established prestige and economic power of the church had a major impact on English country houses. The 1530s saw first the closing down of smaller monastic houses, then all of them (1536–40), with official disconnection of the English church from the Roman papacy in 1536. The dissolution of the monasteries stimulated a great change in landownership and many gentry families were able to extend their estates and build new houses, sometimes using stone from suppressed monasteries, as at Hengrave Hall in Suffolk.

Indeed, some new landlords adapted the lodgings of former monastic complexes to their own use, as at Lacock Abbey in Wiltshire and Beaulieu in Hampshire. The Reformation involved a fundamental shift away from the dominance of ecclesiastical architecture, and also made England a safe haven for Protestant craftsmen from Flanders.

Burghley House, one of the great houses of the Elizabethan age, was built for William Cecil, Elizabeth's Chief Secretary, between the 1550s and 1580s. It combines Classical detail, such as a roofline of paired Classical columns, with self-consciously medieval forms, such as its huge great hall.

By 1592, the writer Francis Bacon noted a building boom:

> There has never been the like number of fair and stately houses as have been
> set up from the ground since her Majesties reign; in so much that there have
> been reckoned in one shire that is not great to the number of two and thirty
> which have all been new built within that time.

RIGHT: *Built around a large courtyard, between 1556
and 1587 for William Cecil, Lord Burghley, Burghley
House in Lincolnshire typifies the powerful architecture
of the later 16th century, combining medieval traditions
with Classical detail, on a scale that still competes with
buildings of any later century.*

RIGHT: *The Little Castle, Bolsover, Derbyshire, built in 1612 for Sir Charles Cavendish (later Duke of Newcastle), illustrates the continuing glamour of the castle style and the persistence of the medieval martial or chivalric tradition, although it combines Classical detail within.*

FAR RIGHT: *Ashdown House, Berkshire, is a handsome 1660s hunting lodge in the Classical tradition with hipped roof and central lantern, and symmetrical pavilion wings (thought to have been designed by William Winde). Its height and the roof balustrade reflect the custom of watching the chase over treetops.*

Other great houses of the age share the same massive physical presence, lively skyline and impressive banks of windows, particularly those, such as Hardwick Hall, designed by the mason Robert Smythson, effectively the first well-documented English architect. Fine examples of the type include Longleat in Wiltshire and Wollaton in Nottingham.

Hardwick Hall also showed a variation on the courtyard plan of many houses of the period, being arranged in grand storeys, with a vast long gallery on top and a great chamber and bedchamber below, along with a central hall and further everyday living rooms on the ground floor. Such grand and expansive designs expressed the confidence and invention of the era.

Some great houses were designed to entertain the monarch and his retinue. In similar vein, lesser gentry houses reflected the taste, if not the scale, of the local great houses. It is interesting to note the stylistic influence of great houses on lesser gentry dwellings roundabout.

THE TRIUMPH OF THE CLASSICAL

THE EARLY SEVENTEENTH CENTURY also saw the building and rebuilding of many smaller manor houses, as well as houses of unusual poetry, such as the Little Castle at Bolsover in Derbyshire, with its richly appointed interiors (designed by John Smythson, son of Robert).

It is extraordinary, however, to realize that the same decade that produced the beautiful crenellated Little Castle at Bolsover should also have seen the erection of the most innovative and influential Classical building in Britain: the Queen's House in Greenwich, designed in 1616–19 by Inigo Jones for James I's wife, Queen Anne of Denmark, and completed in the 1630s for Queen Henrietta Maria, wife to James's son, Charles I.

Jones is a key figure in the story of English architecture: he had travelled in Italy and studied the survivals of the architecture of ancient Rome, such as the surviving fragments of temples and columns. Jones had seen things at first hand which his predecessors had seen only as engravings. In the Veneto around Venice, Jones also saw the sixteenth-century villas of the Renaissance architects Andrea Palladio and Vincenzo Scammozzi, who sought to revive the stately architecture of ancient Rome.

A designer of court masques (in which masked performers danced and acted), Jones was also surveyor-general to the King's Works. The Queen's House was, as Jones himself wrote, 'solid, proporsionable and according to the rules'. By 'rules', he meant the Classical rules originally laid down by the ancient Roman authors, such as Vitruvius, and later published by Andrea Palladio in his *I Quatro Libri dell'Architettura* [*Four Books of Architecture*] (1570). Along with Jones's designs for Whitehall Palace in London, of which only the Banqueting House was built, the Queen's House started a revolution.

For obvious reasons the other revolution, the mid-seventeenth-century Civil War between King Charles I and Parliament, created something of a slow-down in country house building, but did not divert the inexorable architectural impetus towards Classicism. Both the Queen's House and Wilton in Wiltshire, on which Inigo Jones is thought to have advised in the 1630s at the suggestion of Charles I, were flat-roofed in the Classical manner.

The Classical elevation, combined with the more familiar pitched roof of our northern tradition (better suited to rain), created a Classical hybrid, as at Coleshill in Berkshire (sadly demolished) and Ashdown in Berkshire. These prim, handsome houses were popular in the

decades after the Restoration, when some of the most elegant and refined buildings in England were produced. Belton House in Lincolnshire is a wonderful example, well-proportioned, with two principal floors of equal height, raised over a basement. It was built on an H-shape with double-room width in the centre (technically known as double pile, as earlier houses were more often single-room width, or single pile), and the main entrance marked with a Classical pediment. The same pattern was repeated on a smaller scale throughout the country.

The interiors of these late seventeenth- and early eighteenth-century country houses were richly decorated with carving by (or in the manner of) Grinling Gibbons and lively plasterwork ceilings. The original furnishings would have been richly upholstered in velvets, with Dutch and oriental ceramics on display. This was also the era when sash windows first arrived to become such a distinctive feature in country house architecture.

With the image of these houses in mind, one can well understand the story told by Daniel Defoe about William III, in his book: *The Compleat English Gentleman* (1730s):

LEFT: *A classic Restoration house built in the 1680s for Sir John Brownlow, Belton House in Lincolnshire is handsomely proportioned and equally handsomely detailed, with a typically low-pitched roof and central lantern under a cupola.*

The late ever Glorious King William us'd frequently to say that, if he was not a king, and Providence had mercifully plac'd his station of life in his choice, he would be an English gentleman of two thousand pounds a year.

Some country houses, such as Dyrham Park in Gloucestershire, were built or rebuilt at this time the better to receive and entertain the monarch and his retinue. The influence of the court style of the French King Louis XIV also contributed to the fashion of laying out a country house with formal apartments. Each apartment, with its dedicated set of usually rather tall rooms, would be connected by a suite of doors all lined up, creating the supremely grand interior effect known as an *enfilade*.

The generation of Sir Christopher Wren produced some of the most memorable country houses. Although Wren added the west front to Hampton Court and designed Kensington Palace he apparently did little documented country-house work. The period from the 1690s to 1720s, sometimes called the English Baroque, was characterized by a dramatic sense of

RIGHT: *One of the finest expressions of the English Baroque, Castle Howard in Yorkshire was designed in 1699 for the 3rd Earl of Carlisle by the playwright-turned-architect John Vanbrugh and his assistant, Nicholas Hawksmoor. Crowned with an elegant dome, it is every inch a palace.*

movement and illusionistic space – the Baroque style emerged in Rome with the architecture of Francesco Borromini and Gian Bernini.

ENGLISH PALACES: BAROQUE TO PALLADIAN

JOHN VANBRUGH, soldier and playwright-turned-architect, designed Blenheim Palace in Oxfordshire for the Duke of Marlborough, around 1705. Chatsworth in Derbyshire was also rebuilt *c.* 1700–1705. The second stage was carried out by William Talman and Nicholas Hawksmoor, brilliant assistant to both Wren and Vanbrugh, who built the jewel-like Easton Neston, in Northamptonshire. Such buildings spoke of the supreme self-confidence of the age.

Many of the finest interiors of these great houses were richly painted with figurative scenes by artists such as Antonio Verrio, who also painted the rooms created by Talman at Burghley House in Lincolnshire, notably the Heaven Room.

But as so often happens in fashion, just as the English Baroque became really interesting, it became unfashionable. Architects of the younger generation, including the aristocratic amateur Richard Boyle, the 3rd Earl of Burlington, William Kent and Colen Campbell, started the Palladian Revival, which looked back to the Palladian designs of Inigo Jones, inspired by the Italian villas of Andrea Palladio, which, in turn, were modelled on ancient Roman villas.

The Palladian style was championed in a number of publications, including Vitruvius's *Britannicus* (1715) published by Colen Campbell, and Palladio's own *I Quatro Libri dell'Architettura* (1570) (see page 25). Lord Burlington, with Kent, designed Chiswick House, based on Palladio's Villa Capra, while Campbell designed Stourhead House in Wiltshire, based on the Villa Emo.

The great houses of the Palladian revival were powerful symbols of the significant role of the aristocracy after the Hanoverian succession of George I in 1714. Holkham Hall in Norfolk, built in 1734, is one of the greatest statements of the Anglo-Palladian country house. Kent provided initial designs, the patron Thomas Coke, 1st Earl of Leicester, employed Mathew Brettingham as architect, and apparently made not a few design decisions himself.

LEFT: *A typical medium-sized Georgian villa of the mid-18th century, Barlaston Hall in Staffordshire was designed by Sir Robert Taylor. Compact and elegant, it is raised up on a basement with a circuit of rooms surrounding a central staircase hall. Windows on every side enjoy views over the landscape.*

The typical English Palladian country house is entered through a great portico, which led into a grand entrance hall, usually, as at Holkham, austerely Classical in character. This led in turn to a *piano nobile* (or principal ground floor raised over a basement, known as a rustic) with all the grander rooms for entertaining.

The austerity and ornamental plainness of the Palladian exterior is worth noting. The early eighteenth-century architect Robert Morris put it thus:

> *…a building, well proportioned, without Dress, will ever please; as a plain Coat may fit as graceful and easy, on a well-proportioned Man … But if you will be lavish in your Ornament, your structure will look rather like a Fop, with a superfluity of gaudy Tinsel, than real decoration.*

However, in many of the great English Palladian country houses, such as Mereworth Castle in Kent, the outer austerity contrasts with the extraordinary decorative richness within. The interiors of the 1720s and 1730s included great plasterwork ceilings created by itinerant Italian plaster workers, known as the stuccadores, who specialized in figure decoration, such as the naked gods and goddesses of Classical mythology.

THE GEORGIAN GENT: HEIR OF EMPIRE

THE CHARACTER AND contents of the mid-eighteenth century country house were directly linked to the Grand Tour, a period of travel, based around the major Italian cities, especially Rome. The tour became an indispensable feature of the education of any young English gentleman or nobleman of independent means, until the end of the eighteenth century.

Not only did the tour develop familiarity with the great buildings of the Classical world (as they survived in ruins in Rome), but it also encouraged the collecting bug. Most English Grand Tourists of wealth collected some Italian paintings and Classical sculpture, as illustrated by such glorious rooms as the Sculpture Gallery at Holkham Hall.

RIGHT: *The Picturesque, castellated outline of Belvoir Castle, Rutland (seat of the Dukes of Rutland), was remodelled in the early 19th century to create an ever more Romantic image of the castle's 'Saxon' origins. The richly appointed interiors were designed in contrasting character by Mathew Wyatt and Sir John Thoroton.*

England was enjoying a period of unprecedented political stability after all the upheavals of the later seventeenth century, and an economic boom and territorial expansion across the waters. It is easy to see how the eighteenth-century English aristocracy saw themselves almost as heirs to the lost Roman Empire and Classical civilization.

In the 1750s and 1760s the Palladian villa evolved in a new direction, more in the spirit of a suburban retreat, ideal for entertaining on the edge of London, such as Danson House, near Bexleyheath. At the same time, smaller, more compact country seats were created in the style of these suburban villas such as Barlaston Hall. The plan of Robert Taylor's Harleyford Manor in Buckinghamshire, for instance, had a drawing room, dining room and library on the main floor, and a first floor of bedrooms, all around a top-lit staircase hall.

Architects such as Sir William Chambers, Sir Robert Taylor and John Carr of York provided numerous houses of the type, handsome, medium-sized Classical boxes. By contrast, the great Palladian palaces were, by the late eighteenth century, considered, as the diarist Mrs Lybbe Powys once said (rather harshly) of Holkham Hall: 'too grand and too gloomy, and what I style most magnificently uncomfortable'.

The mid-eighteenth century also saw two other twists of taste, which had a huge impact on the country house and the way it was designed. The first, in reaction to the perceived heaviness of Palladian style, affected the interior, which burst into a lively display of Rococo decor, encompassing both oriental chinoiserie and light-hearted Gothic styles. The Chinese taste is beautifully, if eccentrically, illustrated in the Chinese Tea Alcove at Claydon House in Buckinghamshire; while fine examples of Gothic Rococo can be seen at Horace Walpole's Strawberry Hill in Middlesex, and at Arbury Hall in Warwickshire.

The other twist in style was felt outside, with the development of the landscape park, associated with the name of Lancelot 'Capability' Brown. Brown and his imitators transformed the settings of many country houses into seemingly wild landscapes, with massive new plantings of trees and the creation of great new lakes. In the later eighteenth century the principle of the Picturesque, with its emphasis on pleasing irregularity in landscape, added to a growing enthusiasm for Gothic

architecture. Both shifts in style help to explain the eventual development of country house architecture during the course of the nineteenth century.

But first another great wave of Classicism shaped country house design. Sometimes called the neo-Classical style, it was more directly modelled on Classical prototypes. This is associated with the work of the ubiquitous Scottish-born designer Robert Adam, who brought a highly professional approach to the planning of the country house and town house.

In particular Adam cultivated a new decorative style (sometimes called Etruscan), light and restrained by comparison to the decoration of the previous generations, and more self-consciously Classical, as based on new archaeological discoveries about genuine Roman decoration. Adam also designed all the decoration and furnishings in the same spirit. The finest examples of his work include Osterley Park and Syon House, both in Middlesex, Saltram in Devon and Kedleston Hall in Derbyshire (although Dr Johnson thought its dazzling Marble Hall too large, saying it 'would do excellently for a town hall').

By the early 1800s, the dominance of Classical design was beginning to be challenged by a taste for old English styles, which had nationalist overtones, at a time when the country was at war with France. While some patrons continued to build impressively weighty neo-Classical houses, such as Belsay Hall in Northumberland (inspired by Ancient Greece), other patrons demanded designs that evoked the Picturesque country houses of the sixteenth and seventeenth centuries or the more

Romantic castles of the Middle Ages. Examples of charming castellated piles of this age include Smirke's Eastnor Castle in Herefordshire and Wyatt's rambling Ashridge in Hertfordshire, as well as the bold turrets of Belvoir Castle in Rutland (intended to evoke 'Saxon' architecture); the latter's interiors are perhaps the finest expositions of Regency taste in England. John Nash, who designed Italianate Cronkhill, near Shrewsbury, and the Indian-style Brighton Pavilion, could also oblige a patron either in the Jacobean or castle style.

The Picturesque quality of such houses seems to have been a result, partly, of their informality of composition, which in turn was reflected in a less formal arrangement of rooms within the

LEFT: *Scarisbrick Hall, Lancashire, a richly detailed*
house of the late 1830s and 1840s, was designed by
A. W. N. Pugin for Catholic landowner Charles
Scarisbrick. With its vast great hall and clock tower,
Scarisbrick illustrates the full vigour of Pugin's
remarkable advocacy of the Gothic Revival.

READING
A COUNTRY HOUSE

house. The architect and landscape gardener Humphry Repton encouraged a new attitude to the relationship of the garden and the house, illustrated by the popularity of the conservatory.

The variety of style available to the country house builder (whether building afresh or renewing an old seat) in the nineteenth century is disconcerting to modern eyes. The architect Robert Kerr wrote in *The Gentleman's House* (1864): 'A bewildered gentleman may venture to suggest that he wants only a simple comfortable house, in no style at all – except the comfortable style, if there be one', and continued:

> *The architect agrees; but they are all comfortable. 'Sir you are the paymaster,*
> *and must therefore be pattern-master; you choose the style of your house as you*
> *choose the build of your hat; – you can have Classical, columnar or non-*
> *Columnar, arcuated or trabeated, rural or civil or indeed palatial, you can*
> *have Elizabethan in equal variety, Renaissance ditto, or . . . Medieval in any*
> *one of many periods and many phases – old English, French, German,*
> *Belgian, Italian and more.*

The successful industrialist and imperial trader embraced the attractions of country estate ownership with remarkable enthusiasm and poured great funds into land purchase and the building of country houses. Until the 1870s the country estate represented a good investment, as agriculture was then profitable. Landownership also guaranteed some sort of social position and prestige (and an escape from the grime of the industrial cities and ports where their money was made). It is a world described well in the novels of Trollope.

A central theme of Victorian country-house design was the celebration of 'Old England', and the allied advocacy of the Gothic by architects such as A. W. N. Pugin and George Gilbert Scott. The baronial (or Old Scotland) style of William Burn ran parallel. Traditional land-owning families, often boosted by the profits of coal-mining or property development in the cities or a useful marriage into one of these territories, also rebuilt their houses in up-to-date fashions.

BELOW: *Rodmarton Manor, Gloucestershire, an early 20th-century monument to the values of the Arts and Crafts movement, was designed by Ernest Barnsley in 1909 and completed in 1929.*

RIGHT: *A great Victorian mansion, Bayons Manor, Lincolnshire, was built in 1836–42 by Charles Tennyson d'Eyncourt for himself. Having fallen into disrepair it was demolished in 1964.*

Rebuilding or remodelling and extending, was pursued not least to embrace available new technologies, including electricity, which promised increased comforts for the family by the end of the century. Many country houses received extensive additions in the nineteenth century, with elaborately specialized service quarters.

The Victorian age also saw a shift in social perspective that impressed moral and social obligations on landowners. Victorian morality was manifested in separate zones for male and female unmarried guests and also for servants, as well as in the rebuilding of parish churches, the founding of village schools and, in some cases, the improvement of tenants' cottages.

By the 1870s, architects such as Richard Norman Shaw were rediscovering the delights of the red-brick house of the late seventeenth and early eighteenth centuries, creating a style that became known as the Queen Anne Revival. The last decades of the nineteenth century saw the start of the dazzling career of Edwin Lutyens, whose early country houses were inspired by the pretty older manor houses of south-west Surrey, but whose designs in the 1920s and 1930s

RIGHT: *A new neo-Classical country house, Wakeham in Sussex was designed around solar energy principles by Robert Adam.*

represented a full-blooded return to ideals of Georgian grandeur. Lutyens' clients were often bankers and industrialists rather than traditional landowners.

The 1880s to the 1920s was also the period of some very high-minded Arts and Crafts architecture, in which the qualities of hand craftsmanship were particularly celebrated in reaction to 'copyist' or 'historicist' nineteenth-century architecture, of which Rodmarton Manor in Gloucestershire is such a good example. A parallel movement in the early decades of the twentieth century was the rediscovery and restoration of old manor houses (such as Westwood Manor in Wiltshire).

COUNTRY HOUSES IN THE TWENTIETH CENTURY: A CHANGING WORLD

THE FIRST DECADE of the twentieth century was the last great age of country house building, rebuilding and extending, as exemplified by West Dean in Sussex. The period was a high watermark of comfort and grandeur. In 1905, in his *English Hours*, Henry James described Wroxton Abbey: 'everything that in the material line can render life noble and charming has been gathered into it with a profusion that makes the whole place a monument to past opportunity'.

But almost immediately the future of these houses, and their way of life, changed irrevocably with World War I, not least because the trading bloc formerly enjoyed by the British Empire had began to unravel. The numbers employed in domestic service also dropped rapidly during these years.

During World War II, most country houses of any size were pressed into some sort of service, as military bases, hospitals, homes for evacuated schools or refugees. Many landowners returned to find their ancestral houses in a bad condition, and others saw no future in the way of life such houses represented, as they began to be seriously hit by death duties and taxation under the new tax laws.

In this period many houses were sold, converted or simply demolished. It is a tale told with some force by John Harris in *No Voice from the Hall* (1999). The Victoria and Albert Museum's 1974 exhibition on the *Destruction of the Country House*, in which Harris, Marcus Binney and Roy Strong all played critical roles, marked an important shift in public opinion. By the end of that decade the demolition of a country house of architectural quality began to be regarded as the equivalent of burning an old master painting from the National Gallery.

New country houses continued to be built throughout the twentieth century, some as adaptations of earlier houses, and some as replacements. New country house design has flirted with International Modernism, one famous example being the rebuilding of Eaton Hall in Cheshire, itself now remodelled in a traditional style. Many country houses built since World War II have followed a loosely Classical tradition. Not surprisingly, they are universally smaller than the houses built up to World War I, more in that villa tradition of the mid-eighteenth century.

John Outram's house in Sussex, built for the Rausing family, is a work of rare boldness and colour, and Sebastian de Ferranti's remarkable 1980s Henbury Hall in Cheshire is a Palladian

homage. Other architects of note in the field of new Classical country house building include the late Raymond Erith, Quinlan Terry and Robert Adam, whose Wakeham in Sussex, built on principles of solar heating, shows how important environmental thinking is to architects today.

But it is perhaps the survival of the historic country house that is the great achievement of the later twentieth century. Indeed it is probably the development of the astonishing skills of conservation and restoration that may be recognized as the defining architectural legacy of the 1990s and early twenty-first century. Such are the skills that were used to rebuild Uppark in Sussex, after the fire, and at Hampton Court and Windsor Castle after their respective fires.

There is also a list of country houses that were sold or leased away by landowning families, which have been reinhabited, such as the Earl of Feversham's Duncombe Park in Yorkshire or the Earl of Derby's Knowsley Hall in Derbyshire. Most major landowners with historic houses in their possession take seriously the responsibility to preserve the great masterpieces in their care, and open them to the public. These include Hatfield House in Hertfordshire, Arundel Castle in Sussex, Woburn in Bedfordshire and Harewood House in Yorkshire, to name just a few.

LEFT: *Beautifully restored after a devastating fire in 1989, the late 17th-century house Uppark in Sussex is a monument to contemporary conservation and craft skills.*

READING
A COUNTRY HOUSE

The National Trust has also rescued and preserved hundreds of fine houses, setting exemplary standards of preservation and presentation, from Ightham Mote in Kent to Attingham Park in Shropshire, from Kedleston Hall in Derby to Tatton Park in Cheshire, from Plas Newydd on Anglesey to Tyntesfield in Somerset. The list of country houses in their care is breathtaking, encompassing examples from every important period. It may be that in some cases the Trust can seem over-protective, but it should be remembered that preservation is the Trust's first duty.

It is perhaps Chatsworth in Derbyshire that best sums up the achievement of some traditional landowning families in turning around the fortunes of great hulks of houses for which few saw a future in the 1940s and 1950s. Originally an Elizabethan country house, Chatsworth was transformed in the 1690s into a Baroque palace and considerably extended in the early nineteenth century. The late Duke of Devonshire had to deal with devastating death duties in the 1950s. The house had been used by an evacuated school in the war, and it was some time before the family eventually decided to move back in. The tax bill was settled partly by handing over Hardwick Hall to the nation in lieu of tax. The late Duke and his Duchess, the present dowager, Deborah, then sorted out the decoration, interpretation and presentation of this great ducal palace, with admirable enthusiasm, which has made Chatsworth a byword in the survival and revival of the English country house.

Chatsworth is now vested in a charitable trust, but is still occupied by the family for whom it was built, a centre of private and public hospitality, of the preservation of the relics of the past and the continued patronage of the arts. To family portraits by Thomas Gainsborough have been added ones by Lucian Freud and Stephen Conroy. The best bit of this story is somehow the personable, family quality of Chatsworth, the blunt acknowledgement by the family of the privilege they enjoy, matched by their pleasure in sharing it with the public.

Country houses of all sizes have been visited by a curious public for centuries, probably from earliest times – the first manor house complexes were, in some sense, seen as public buildings. Certainly there are hundreds and hundreds of country houses to visit and enjoy in your own personal way. I hope this book is a useful and pleasant companion on those journeys.

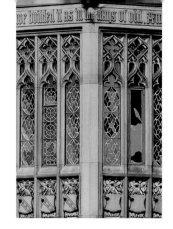

CHAPTER ONE
READING THE OUTSIDE

The Country House at First Sight

HAVE YOU EVER CAUGHT a glimpse of a country house at a distance, and been struck by the shape it creates on the landscape, as if it had been composed, like a picture, against the setting sun or early morning mist? For that matter have you ever glimpsed Hardwick Hall or Little Castle Bolsover in Derbyshire from the M1 and thought what extraordinary silhouettes they possess? Or turned down a little road near Aylsham in Norfolk and spied the stately but somehow cheerful symmetry of Blickling Hall?

In many ways the most distinctive element of a country house of any period is its outline, the effect created by the whole structure and particularly the shape of the house and overall incident

LEFT: *The lively roofline at East Barsham Manor, Norfolk, was built in the early 16th century for Sir Henry Fermor. The castellated composition, topped with twisted chimneys, crenellation, turrets and the pinnacles of a castle, nonetheless remains emphatically domestic in character.*

of the roof. The outline or silhouette was clearly a considered part of the design process, not least in early fortified buildings, whether built to be strong and impregnable, such as the Norman Tower of London, or to impress with might and magnificence, such as the great castles of the fourteenth and fifteenth centuries, Bodiam and Herstmonceux in Sussex. With their emphatic symmetry of towers and central gatehouse, such castles were ambitious showpieces, celebrating status and knightly virtue, as much as military might. The very act of crenellation, indeed, licensed by the crown, was a recognition of social position.

MEDIEVAL TO ELIZABETHAN: BUSY ROOFLINES AND EVENTFUL SKYLINES

IN THE CASE OF the medieval manor house, the overall outline always illuminates the hierarchy of buildings in the manor complex. The great hall is usually marked out by the very expanse of its roof within a courtyard or group of related buildings. Even in relatively small manor houses, such as Cothay Manor in Somerset, the unbroken presence of the steeply pitched roof immediately indicates the presence of a large hall, while at the same time proclaiming the status of the owner.

When approaching an early Tudor or Elizabethan house, one cannot fail to notice how self-consciously lively and 'busy' the rooflines are. The crenellations and highly decorated brick chimneys and pepper-pot shaped pinnacles of, for instance, East Barsham Manor in Norfolk of the 1520s exemplify the period's overt courtly chivalry. The pepper-pot turrets of Tudor and Elizabethan houses probably originated in the palaces of Henry VIII at Richmond and Nonesuch in Surrey, but also, particularly at a distance, still had something of the fortress about them.

The taste for balanced, symmetrical elevations seen in some early Tudor houses, such as Sutton Place in Surrey, became more notable in the great houses of the Elizabethan and Jacobean eras (for example Montacute House in Somerset and Bramshill House in Hampshire). These rather massive and heavy buildings, disposed in solid E-, H- or U-shaped plans, have immensely lively rooflines with strong repeated vertical elements, such as curved or triangular

ABOVE: *The picture of an English castle, Herstmonceux Castle, Sussex, possesses unusual drama in its unprecedented symmetrical façade. A splendid showpiece in its day, it was built in brick by Sir Roger Fiennes, Treasurer to the Household (1439–48), at a time when brick, still imported from Flanders, was in itself an expression of status.*

LEFT: *Once the visitor has passed through the gatehouse of Cothay Manor, Somerset, the presence of the steep unbroken roof of this handsome late 15th-century manor house immediately declares the status of the building.*

RIGHT: *In the late 16th and early 17th centuries tall chimney stacks contributed to the lively roofline of country houses.*

gables (or both), topped with finials, or obelisks, and combined with emphatic chimneys, sometimes in stone but more often in brick.

The typical shapely swirled (barley-sugar-style) red-brick chimney stack associated with the later sixteenth century was certainly valued for its visual impact. At Framlingham Castle in Suffolk many of the stacks added in the 1570s were apparently never functional but were felt to enhance the prestigious outline of the castle walls. The Jacobean chimney tended to be slightly less ornate, but still tall and often set at an angle, with a decorative cap.

Many great late sixteenth-century houses made an especial virtue of their expanse of roof by creating flat walkways, such as can be seen at Longleat in Wiltshire and at Burghley House in Lincolnshire. On the rooftop walkways, family and guests could promenade, admire the view of landed possession, and marvel at the family's ingenuity. Both Longleat and Burghley offer wonderfully fanciful rooftop Arcadian fairylands, with chimneys like Classical columns (and, at Burghley, Classical obelisks and a pyramid-shaped clock tower). Both houses, from a distance, present a complex and fantastical front.

It had also become the fashion to take pudding (known then as the banqueting course) in a specially built banqueting (literally, pudding) house in the garden or on the roof. The great roofs of Burghley, Longleat and Hardwick Hall all have rooms, at roof level, capable of holding sweet treats.

JACOBEAN TO LATE STUART: ORNAMENTAL SYMMETRY

DURING THE SEVENTEENTH CENTURY, repeated gables – semi-circular or topped with a triangular pediment – as well as the obligatory tall chimneys played an important part in the typically balanced elevation of early seventeenth-century country houses, such as Hatfield House in Hertfordshire and Blickling Hall in Norfolk. From the middle of the century, with the influence of Inigo Jones, the overall effect became more sober, the house seen as more of a rectangle.

The outlines of the more Classically informed elevations of the delicious country houses of the later seventeenth century show an emphatic alteration in the treatment of the roofline involving the

rectangle, hipped roof and central domed lantern. Given the wet climate in England, Classically flat roofs were not ideal. Instead, a version of the hipped roof emerged, based on the Dutch pitched model, which contributed to the now very familiar outline of the typical Restoration manor house, as at the demolished Coleshill, Berkshire, and Winslow Hall in Buckinghamshire.

The central lantern under a cupola (or small dome) sometimes served as an entrance point to the roof, as well as providing a good central focus to the composition aligned over the entrance door. The windows of the attic floor, the dormers, also helped to create an overall feeling of symmetry and orderliness, often with a triangular or curved pediment.

From this time a key element in the overall outline of a house would be the use of a low-pitched triangular pediment giving a central emphasis to the main façade. Above the pediment, the roofline was usually topped with tall Classical chimneys, in brick or stone, designed to give an appearance of being panelled. Many larger country houses of the period had a walkway on top railed around with a balustrade. Sometimes one spots paintings of late seventeenth-century country houses showing people gathered on the roof looking over the balustrade like trippers on a seaside pier.

LEFT: *Blickling Hall, Norfolk, presents a lively gabled outline, typical of the later Elizabethan and Jacobean country house. Built in 1619–20, it was designed by the carpenter Robert Lyminge, who also created the Jacobean showpiece Hatfield House in Hertfordshire.*

BELOW: *One of the first of its type, the roofline at mid-17th-century Coleshill, Berkshire, was designed with pitched roof, dormers, a domed lantern and emphatic panelled chimney stacks. Coleshill was demolished in the 1950s.*

RIGHT: *At Seaton Delaval Hall, Northumberland, the bold recessions of towers, pediments and columns are typical of the English Baroque of John Vanbrugh.*

Some later seventeenth-century houses were designed on the Italian model with a lower-pitched roof behind a balustrade (as at Dyrham Park in Gloucestershire), which set the pattern for a good number of early eighteenth-century country houses. Chimneystacks become a less distinctive feature, although they remained symmetrically arranged contributing to the overall effect.

The late seventeenth century also saw great architectural adventures at Castle Howard in Yorkshire and Blenheim Palace in Oxfordshire, with their almost unbelievably eventful skylines, designed by John Vanbrugh, assisted by Nicholas Hawksmoor. While Castle Howard evoked the glamour of the Classical Mediterranean world, Blenheim harked back to the self-conscious and glamorous rooflines of the great Elizabethan houses, such as Wollaton Hall in Nottingham and Burghley House in Lincolnshire, in a bold gesture of nationalism.

GEORGIAN TO REGENCY: FROM TEMPLES BACK TO TURRETS

FROM THE EARLY eighteenth century the Classicizing influence of the architect Richard Boyle, 3rd Earl of Burlington, and fellow architects inspired by the Classical designs of the Venetian Renaissance architect Andrea Palladio and his English disciple, Inigo Jones, had a rather sobering effect on the country house outline. Although Burlington and his colleagues designed some charming domes, at Chiswick House and Mereworth Castle in Kent, most Anglo-Palladian country houses had defiantly flat roofs, with a parapet screening a deliberately low-pitched roof.

During the eighteenth century, the temple front became a typical detail for many new country houses, either with a projecting portico or with a large pediment designed into the main

elevation, again giving a central point to the overall composition. Some Anglo-Palladian country houses, such as Holkham Hall in Norfolk, achieved a surprising varied roofline, with a central pediment, square corner towers and four balancing wings.

It is during the early Gothic Revival, associated with the light-hearted and decorative Rococo taste of the 1750s and 1760s, that the country house architect defiantly recaptured the pleasures of the earlier vivid outline and self-conscious chivalric confections of the Elizabethan and Jacobean eras.

Examples abound, from Horace Walpole's house at Strawberry Hill in Twickenham, to the bold castle-style houses designed by James Wyatt and Robert Adam. The Prince Regent's

ABOVE: *A fine, red-sandstone house, Berrington Hall in Shropshire was designed by Henry Holland in the late 1770s for the Honourable Thomas Harley. Its massive Ionic portico illustrates both the continuity of the Classical pattern and also the reduction of the basement level. The service quarters are situated in an adjoining service wing.*

LEFT: *Hagley Hall, Worcestershire, built in the 1750s for the 1st Lord Lyttleton, clearly illustrates the Palladian style. Note the characteristic outline and roofline, formed essentially from a large rectangle, with a central pediment, a flat roof behind a balustrade and four corner towers with pyramidal roofs.*

favourite architect, John Nash, produced several fine country houses, often deliberately asymmetrical, such as the castellated Caerhays Castle in Cornwall, or the Italian-style Cronkhill in Shropshire; the latter, with its round tower and arcade, recalled a farmhouse on the Italian campagna, as depicted in the paintings of Claude Lorrain.

Whatever style was chosen by Nash's patrons, asymmetry was the key, and a sense of fitting into the landscape as if into a painting. The overall effect, much admired by the watercolourists, is of a happy lop-sidedness, evoking older houses that had grown piecemeal into pleasing shapes, well settled into their landscape. A good example survives at Scotney Castle in Kent, with its gables and turreted mixture of Elizabethan and Jacobean styles.

RIGHT: *Originally an 18th-century house, Highclere Castle, Hampshire, was completely remodelled in the 1830s and 1840s in a Romantic Elizabethan style by Charles Barry, who created its Picturesque roofline, with the detail and variety so valued by many Victorian patrons and designers.*

VICTORIAN TO MODERN: GOTHS AND MODS

WITH THE NINETEENTH-CENTURY country house, the outline and overall shape became as varied as the architectural sources. What did emerge as the keynote of the Victorian country house, however, was its distinct variety of roofline. Typically vivid and 'busy' rooflines were seen everywhere, from Lord Lytton's Knebworth House in Hertfordshire and Sir Charles Barry's Highclere Castle in Berkshire, remodelled in the Elizabethan style, to Baron Ferdinand de Rothschild's extravagantly French-château-style Waddesdon Manor in Buckinghamshire.

By the 1870s Richard Norman Shaw was designing pleasing houses in the pretty, red-brick Queen Anne Revival style as well. There was therefore something of a recovery of the Classical model, sometimes with symmetrical wings, as at Bryanston in Dorset, a trend that continued throughout the Edwardian era, for instance in the work of Reginald Blomfield, and well into the 1930s.

The innovative late nineteenth- and early twentieth-century architect, Edwin Lutyens, who began in the Arts and Crafts enthusiasm for well-built smaller manor houses and larger farm houses, produced a great variety of styles in his career ranging from early roofs of massive steep pitches (as at Little Thakeham in Sussex), evoking the old houses of the south-east of England, and roofs with alert, twisted chimneys of the Elizabethan/Jacobean sort (as at Marsh Court in Hampshire) to Lutyens' later roofs of self-conscious Classical formality (as at Gledstone Hall in Yorkshire).

From the 1930s through to the 1960s, some new smaller country houses were designed with the flat roofs of International Modernism, but probably, since the 1930s, more country houses were instead designed in versions and variations of the compact Georgian-villa style.

The overall outline of a country house may not of course reveal the whole story, but it never fails to offer certain clues. Above all, any excuse to stop and ponder the main elevation of a country house is, in my view, a good one. Pausing to drink in the overall picture of a country house, set in its surrounding landscape, offers some of best visual experiences in Britain.

DOORS, DOORWAYS & ENTRANCES

Finding the Right Way In

As ONE APPROACHES a country house, after first noticing the overall mass of the building, one naturally looks more closely at the point of entry. Designers, aware of the sequential stages of approach, usually invested the entrance and major exterior doorways with some of the finest and most impressive architectural detail in the house.

NORMAN TO JACOBEAN: DRAMATIC PROGRESSION

THE FEW SURVIVING examples of doorways to eleventh- or twelfth-century manor houses are typically round-headed and often detailed with a bold chevron or zigzag pattern. The wooden doors that originally filled arches would have consisted of planks secured by cross-pieces, although none survives intact.

From the late twelfth century onwards, the round-headed arch gave way to the pointed arch – typical of what is called Gothic architecture. Gothic arched doorways were often further framed by a continuous weather moulding (literally a raised and rounded profile in stone intended to throw water away from the door itself) following the line of the arch.

LEFT: *Cothay Manor in Somerset, built in the 1480s, presents a typical manor-house arrangement, with a gatehouse leading to a porch and then into the great hall 'screens passage'.*

ABOVE: *The door case at Trerice Manor, Cornwall, illustrates the typical flattened top-hat look of Tudor weather moulding.*

RIGHT: *The elegant entrance to the great hall at Kirby Hall in Northamptonshire has handsomely carved Classical pilasters, modelled on patterns from John Shute's* First and Complete Grounds of Architecture *(1563).*

It is worth stressing that in the Middle Ages, a door might be only one element in the staged process of entering a country house. Indeed, the approach to a medieval manor would often be mediated first through a stout gatehouse, recalling castle-like security, such as that at fourteenth-century Cothay Manor in Somerset. After passing through the gatehouse, which was often aligned on the main entrance of the great hall within, a visitor would progress through an inner court, and then often under a porch before entering the hall itself.

At Cothay, and elsewhere, this staggered approach had (and still has) the effect of creating a sense of dramatic progression and at the same time providing a certain amount of security and weather protection within. Sometimes the main entrance door itself might contain a smaller door for everyday use, known as a wicket gate, as can be seen at Penshurst Place in Kent.

Most medieval doors were simply made up of two layers of oak planks, with fillets or small ribs over the joins of the planks, studded with nails across the interior support; the nail heads often created a decorative quality on the front. In the fifteenth century principal exterior doors would often be additionally adorned with applied Gothic arched 'tracery' patterns, similar to Gothic traceried windows. During the sixteenth century, the planked door gave way to a more familiar form, which was framed and panelled, with the inner panels pegged into a sturdy framework.

The early sixteenth-century Tudor doorway, like the Tudor window (see page 69), is characterized by a shallow broad arch within a square-headed frame (not unlike a flattened top hat), as at Hampton Court and Sutton Place in Surrey. This door type remained typical for most of the sixteenth century, its shallow arches characteristic of Perpendicular Gothic. The door's weather moulding often formed a square frame over the top, which in turn created a triangular space for decoration, known technically as the spandrel, offering scope for carved decoration, usually of a floral or armorial kind.

From the early sixteenth century, the aesthetic values of the Renaissance revival of interest in Classical culture encouraged the inclusion of details drawn from Roman architecture. Typical Classical detailing emerged in the form of columns or pilasters (flat representations of the column) in the decorative framing of the doorcase or porch, as at Wollaton in Nottinghamshire

and Kirby Hall in Northamptonshire. It was the first period when the Classical column became a major element in the exterior of the English country house, although at first such columns served only as applied decoration.

Some such porches or 'frontispieces' over the main entrance door rise to the full height of the elevation, as at early seventeenth-century Bramshill House in Hampshire, at Hatfield House in Hertfordshire and at Blickling Hall in Norfolk. The theme might be repeated with a sequence of Classical pilasters rising over two or three storeys, emphasizing the dignity and fashion of the place. Such tiers of pilasters are sometimes referred to as a 'tower of the Orders' as they show the three main Classical orders – Doric, Ionic and Corinthian – the most famous example of which is perhaps the entrance to the Bodleian Library in Oxford. The 'order' is the whole gang that makes up the column according to a set formula, including base, shaft and capital, with entablature.

OPPOSITE: *Classical continuity and change.*
(FAR LEFT) *The 1630s door case at Raynham Hall,
Norfolk, illustrates the classic example found in varying
forms throughout the 17th and early 18th centuries, with
the entrance framed by Corinthian pilasters.* (NEAR LEFT)
*Merstham Le Hatch, Kent, has a later Georgian type,
designed by Robert Adam in the 1760s, with a triangular
pediment supported by columns in the Doric order, the
plainest of the Classical orders.*

The lower pilasters would usually be Doric, considered historically the earliest, least decorated and strongest of the orders. The middle Ionic rank was regarded as rather delicate with its scrolled capital. The upper order was usually Corinthian, the most decorative with a capital based on the acanthus leaf. The three orders, which originated in Greek architecture, were adopted by the Romans and widely revived in the Renaissance. It is worth remembering these types of columns and their different orders of decoration and proportion, as they became a key feature of English country house design over the next three centuries.

A simpler version of the main entrance in the Jacobean era was formed by a round-headed arch set between paired columns or pilasters, as at Cold Overton in Lancashire and Fountains Hall in Yorkshire. Sometimes the main entrance was set into a small arcade or loggia, really rather Italian in effect, as at Cranborne Manor in Dorset.

CAROLINE TO GEORGIAN: PUTTING ON A PORTICO

THE ARCHITECTURAL REVOLUTION inspired by Inigo Jones during the 1620s and 1630s set the English country house on a path towards an overall Classical form and proportion, typified by Jones's designs at Queen's House in Greenwich. Jones's deputy, John Webb, went on in 1654 to design a great Corinthian portico at The Vyne in Hampshire, presenting the very image of a Classical Roman temple front.

Such full-height forward-standing porticoes, with columns supporting a great triangular pediment, would became a familiar feature of the eighteenth century, typifying the Georgian country house. But it was at The Vyne in the middle of the seventeenth century that the portico first emerged. Although it took a while for the portico to catch on, a kind of miniature version had developed by the late seventeenth century when most principal doorcases of Classically inspired country houses were neatly framed by Classical columns or pilasters supporting a triangular or curved (segmental) pediment.

Various pattern books, such as Andrea Palladio's *I Quatro Libri dell'Architettura (Four Books on Architecture)* (1570) and James Gibbs' *Book of Architecture* (1728), helped to circulate

different versions of the Palladian patterns for doorcases. Gibbs also promoted the 'correct' system of proportion for Classical columns in his *Rules for Drawing the Several Parts of Architecture* (1725). The cheerily named Batty Langley issued numerous pattern books for builders, including *City and Country Workman's Remembrancer* (1745) and *The Builder's Jewel* (1746), providing useful precedents.

The pediments over doorcases, deliberately recalling the temple or portico roof, were often supported by handsome scrolled or carved brackets. Some pediments, described as 'open', might be left open in the middle with space for a family crest or coat of arms, displaying the owner's status.

The main entrance doors of late seventeenth- and early eighteenth-century country houses were often reached by a shallow flight of steps, underlining the dignity of the approach. From this period doors became framed and panelled with six to eight panels, the number remaining standard throughout the following century. The panels would usually be grained to look like dark wood, or painted in dark colours.

While mid-Georgian doors continued to appear in the established Classical form, some might be round-headed, or include a fan-light or arched window over the door. Later eighteenth- and early nineteenth-century Classical doors tended to be less elaborately detailed.

REGENCY TO EDWARDIAN: MAKING AN ENTRANCE

THE REGENCY COUNTRY house-owner clearly favoured comfort more than his Georgian predecessor and it is common to find a handsome single-storey Classical porch enclosing a main entrance, or leading straight into a small ante-room, while the doorway proper was often treated more plainly. The portico was usually extended outwards in a welcoming fashion to cover a visitor descending from a coach or horse (as at Broughton Hall in Yorkshire); an appealing motif that was perpetuated throughout the nineteenth century.

A key thing to note is that from the Regency period onwards the principal doors of a country house were often part glazed to create a link with the garden and landscape outside, to let more light into the hall, and probably simply to be more welcoming. Many doors of earlier country

LEFT: *Gledstone Hall, Yorkshire, designed by Edwin Lutyens in the 1920s, shows the early 20th-century revival of Classical forms and thus rooflines, although Lutyens' work is perhaps more often associated with handsome country houses designed in Arts-and-Crafts-inspired Old English styles.*

houses were adapted at this time to form glazed doors. By now it was also the norm for the main entrance to be on the ground level.

From the early nineteenth century a renewed interest in historical styles, encouraged by the Gothic Revival, saw a lively return to doors and porches designed in a variety of medieval, Tudor and Jacobean styles, based with greater or lesser attention to detail on models of admired older houses. Houses modelled on the symmetrical elevations of great Elizabethan or Jacobean examples might have a central main entrance, as at Arley Hall in Cheshire, from the 1830s, and Harlaxton Manor in Lincolnshire. Many entrances appear to one side, or at an angle, and often framed by a porch, as at Victorian Tyntesfield in Somerset and Edwardian Sennowe Park in Norfolk.

A return to Classical precedents during the Queen Anne Revival of the 1870s saw many handsome imitations of the late seventeenth- and early eighteenth-century door types, a theme continued in Edwardian country house architecture. In Victorian and Edwardian country houses a handsome and substantial porch played an important part in making the entrance comfortable and welcoming for guests to the legendary house parties of the age.

RIGHT: *The off-centre porch at Standen, Sussex, designed by Philip Webb in the 1880s, illustrates the late Victorian fashion for creating an attractive asymmetry even when using loosely Classical elements. A good example of the Arts and Crafts taste, the door suggests an old farmhouse as much as anything else.*

RIGHT: *The window and interior window seat of the chamber block at the 12th-century Manor House at Boothby Pagnell in Lincolnshire illustrates the typical Norman-style arrangement of paired lights within a larger arch. The lights would always have been fitted with wooden shutters, rather than the later glass seen here.*

WINDOWS

Through the Looking Glass

WHILE A PRINCIPAL door often provides the main visual focus on the front elevation of a house, the many windows of a house are perhaps paramount in their visual effect. As well as providing the vital functional element of letting in light and air, windows form a key aspect in the design and decoration of any country house.

The origin of the word 'window' is uncertain but it has been suggested that it comes from the Old English *vindr* (wind) and *auga* (eye), and it is important to remember that windows provide both light and ventilation. Once again the detailing of a window in a historic country house often reveals useful clues about the original date of the house, and any subsequent periods of alteration.

NORMAN TO TUDOR: LATTICES AND SHUTTERS

THE WINDOWS OF Norman domestic architecture were normally round-arched, as seen at Rochester Castle in Kent. The exterior arch of a Norman window was clearly defined by a raised moulding intended to throw rainwater off the window shutters. A window's moulding was often enriched with deep carving in a chevron or zigzag pattern.

The surviving part of the twelfth-century manor house at Boothby Pagnell in Lincoln-shire, has several original window 'openings', revealing two basic types of domestic window. The more complex type has two round-headed openings or 'lights', framed within a larger arch. Such openings were originally shuttered, rather than glazed, and the grooves – or rebates – for the original shutters can often be seen on the interior of the window. The narrow width of Norman windows provided security – preventing entrance – while also presenting an unmistakable air of structural solidity. The simpler type of window, seen on the ground floor at Boothby, was simply a narrow slit.

The light let in by both types of Norman window was greatly enhanced by the wide splay of the opening, which spread out diagonally from a small opening on the outside to a much larger one within the room's interior. In the few surviving twelfth-century houses, such as Boothby, window seats were incorporated into the interior opening, with a place to lift one's feet off the floor – surely the earliest surviving examples of fitted furniture in the British Isles.

In the thirteenth century the same basic arrangement of narrow paired lights persisted, but by this date the lights were characteristically set in pointed Gothic arches or in three-lobed 'trefoils', sometimes with a small quatrefoil opening above, as seen, for instance, at brick-built Little Wenham Hall in Suffolk. The windows would have been shuttered, although sometimes the small opening above the two arches would be filled with thinly shaved horn to allow some light in.

ABOVE: *Late 15th-century Ockwells Manor, Berkshire, shows the increasing importance of glass in the design of country houses. Note the presence of the armorial stained glass in the main windows of the great hall.*

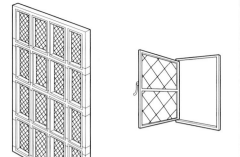

LEFT: *Late 16th-century and early 17th-century windows take the form of stacked-up grids, with a number of small casements (side-opening windows) within.*

In grander houses of the later thirteenth century, the top half of a window might be glazed, with just the lower part shuttered. Glazing would be mostly fixed in position, made up of small diamond panes (or 'quarries') set in diagonal lead frames. The vast majority of glass now present in Gothic windows was inserted at a later date.

Despite the more elaborately carved tracery of fourteenth-century architecture (known as Decorated), the domestic window still followed the basic two-light design, formed from two tall lights divided by an upright mullion and typically crowned with a small opening above.

In the later fourteenth and early sixteenth centuries the status of the more important rooms of a house, the great hall and the great chamber, was usually marked out by the more elaborate windows of the house. In particular the principal end of the great hall, the dais end – where the lord of the manor, his family and higher servants sat at table on a dais – was usually picked out by a great bay window, often called an oriel, although the term was certainly used to describe other projecting windows in the medieval period.

Oriels were well glazed, flooding the dais end with sunlight. Good examples survive at Athelhampton in Dorset and Hengrave Hall in Suffolk, both with handsome fan-vaulted interiors. Oriels were often constructed in the form of projecting three-sided, sometimes multi-sided bays. Some Tudor oriels were so large that they formed, in effect, small side rooms.

In such major windows armorial roundels were often inserted, displaying the family's coat of arms or other heraldic badges, as well as prestigious family connections. Some original examples of armorial glass survive at Ockwells Manor in Berkshire and at Athelhampton in Dorset. At Ockwells Manor the glass had been stored and was put back into its correct position in the early twentieth century. Indeed, much of the armorial stained glass that we encounter today, even in older houses, was installed in the late eighteenth and early nineteenth centuries to re-create the admired effect of surviving examples.

Up to the later sixteenth century, glass was regarded as a movable commodity carried from house to house, until a judgement passed by Sir Edward Coke in 1599 decreed that glass be treated as a fixture.

ELIZABETHAN TO JACOBEAN: GREAT WALLS OF GLASS

IN 1577, THE CLERGYMAN William Harrison wrote an immensely useful book entitled *Description of England*, in which he observed:

> ...of old time our country houses [farmhouses] instead of glass did use much lattice, and that made either of wicker or rifts of oak in checkerwise. I read also that some of the better sort in and before the times of the Saxons ... did make panels of horn instead of glass and fix them in wooden calms. But as horn in windows is now quite laid down in every pleace, so ... our lattices are also grown into less use, because glass is come to be so plentiful.

By the early sixteenth century, the Gothic arrangement of pointed lights framed within a pointed arch had given way to the characteristic Tudor low-arched window, typically a low-flattish arch framed within a square-headed drip-moulding, either singly or in pairs, or stacked up in great windows, typical of the Perpendicular style, of which a fine example appears at Layer Marney Tower in Essex.

Typically at the time, the main weather moulding ran flat across the window, lifting slightly on the return. The surprisingly cheerful effect such windows created in a smaller country house can be seen at fifteenth-century Knook Manor in Wiltshire, the kind of house that makes it clear why nineteenth-century architects found the style so attractive and replicated it so freely across the country.

Later Elizabethan windows dispense with even the arched detail of the Tudor era, becoming in effect flat-headed, but divided into four or six, eight or 12 sections by stone mullions (uprights)

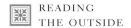
PREVIOUS PAGES: *Tredegar House, Monmouth, built in
the 1660s for William and Blanche Morgan, retains the
cross windows typical of the later 17th-century Classical
house, with a stone mullion and transom, and lead-pane
casements below. In many houses of this period, the cross-
windows were later replaced with sash.*

and transoms (cross-pieces), as seen on the main front of houses such as Montacute in Somerset.
The arrival of foreign master glassmakers, who set up furnaces in England in the 1570s, coupled
with an increase in the supply of glass, contributed to a great fashion for glass in the ambitious
showpiece country houses of the Elizabethan era.

Thus some country houses were then built with the great towering fronts made up of repeated
bays, or just rippling with multiple sectioned windows. The renowned Hardwick Hall in
Derbyshire represents the complete apogee of Tudor glass, about which the rhyme 'Hardwick
Hall/more glass than wall' was quipped. The great bold building just stands there, formed out of
vast glazed grids of stone mullions and transoms, with minimal additional detail. The upper
windows divide into some 16 sections, looking unnervingly modern in certain lights.

Despite the fashion for showing off with glass, the truth is that Tudor windows opened very
little. They were mostly fixed in place, and the panes set in lead. For ventilation, small iron
casements set within the windows opened on hinges. From the accounts of Loseley Park in
Surrey, it is known that glass arrived in crates and glaziers were paid by the hour for their work.
It also appears that a nearly continuous round of repairs was necessary in the larger houses.

In grander houses of the early seventeenth century, many principal windows were rectangular
and divided into four sections by a mullion and transom, forming a type known to historians as
the 'cross-window', as seen on the south front of Hatfield House. The glass within remained
essentially small, composed of squarish panes until the 1660s. Late Elizabethan and Jacobean
glass was often set in very decorative lead framing.

Windows designed by Inigo Jones were glazed with small square panes of glass set in lead, the
window divided horizontally and vertically for strength with cross-pieces and mullions, although
it is interesting that in his architectural drawings Jones tends to leave the cross-piece out. In such
Classical-style cross-windows, the two openings that were usually treated as casements hung on
hinges in the stone or timber mullion, and opened sideways on a scale much more like a modern
window. Although such cross-windows were often replaced by larger sash windows during the
course of the eighteenth century, as can be seen, for instance, on the main front of seventeenth-

LEFT: *Early 17th-century
Blickling Hall, Norfolk, shows
the typical Jacobean grids of
plain stone mullions enclosing
small leaded panes within.
In early 17th-century houses,
the pattern of the glazing leads
is often highly decorative.*

century Kew Palace in Richmond, some cross-windows do survive, as at Tredegar House in Monmouthshire and Ashdown House in Berkshire.

RESTORATION TO VICTORIAN: THE RISE AND RISE OF THE SASH WINDOW

THE WORD 'SASH' derives from the French word *chassis* for frame, although Dr Johnson in his *Dictionary* (1755) wrongly supposed it to come from the word *savoir*, to know, 'a sash window being made particularly for the sake of seeing and being seen'. Although the French had developed a type of sash that needed to be pegged when opened, it seems that the sash window as we know it, operated by a pulley and counterweight system, allowing the sash to remain in any open position, was actually an English innovation. It was probably developed by the Office of Works under Sir Christopher Wren. One French visitor in 1685 described the English innovation of the counterweight sash as 'very convenient and agreeable'.

The 'double-hung' sash window, which so defines the classically inspired country house throughout the whole of the eighteenth century, probably first appeared in England in the 1660s at Charles II's Palace House at Newmarket in Suffolk. It was actually a sash within a cross-window, the window itself being made up of small leaded panes. By the 1680s, counterweight

LEFT: *The sash window entered the scene in the late 17th century and became a dominant feature of Georgian architecture.*

sash windows had certainly been installed in the royal palaces of Whitehall and at St James's; one bill from the royal carpenter, Thomas Kinward, referring to supplying 'very strong sashes, with their frames and brass pulleys' for the Vane Room at Whitehall. The first use of a sash in a country house, however, seems to have been in the later 1680s, at Boughton in Northamptonshire, designed for the 1st Duke of Montagu. From the 1680s onwards sash windows tended to be composed of rectangular panes of crown glass (larger than those at Palace House), set in wooden glazing bars, as in Wren's additions to Hampton Court in the early 1690s. A decade later sash windows were the norm, as shown by the handsome façade of Chicheley Hall in Buckinghamshire of 1719. By the early years of the eighteenth century sash windows were almost universal and had entirely displaced the seventeenth-century cross-window with casements.

By the early eighteenth century, the sash window was usually flush to the elevation, with the sash-boxes, in which the pulleys run, clearly visible. After the London Building Act in 1709, sash boxes had to be set back by 4 inches (10cm), as a fire precaution, which incidentally created a greater feeling of depth in the elevation. The practice, widely adopted throughout the country, was universal by 1750. In 1774 another building act required that sash boxes be concealed within the walls, so that they were no longer exposed at all, which again changed their effect in an elevation.

The verticality of sash windows, symmetrically disposed on an elevation, became one of the key elements in the design of the eighteenth-century country house. The typical arrangement of most eighteenth-century sash windows is of six panes over six panes, but in grander country houses variants of nine over nine, six over nine or nine over six can be found. A common variant

RIGHT: *The elegant façade of Chicheley Hall, Buckinghamshire, was built in 1719–24, by which time the sash window was universally used, although glazing bars were initially quite solid compared to later 18th-century examples. The window surrounds were copied from an Italian pattern book of 1702.*

associated with the work of the Wyatt dynasty of architects is the three-part window, where a central window is balanced by two thin windows of equal height.

While the earliest sash windows had quite heavy glazing bars and squarish panes of glass, the size of individual windowpanes increased as the eighteenth century progressed and techniques of glass production improved.

Over the course of the eighteenth century glazing bars became increasingly fine, as can be seen in the houses designed by Robert Adam during the 1760s, such as Osterley Park in Middlesex or Kedleston Hall in Derbyshire. Also whereas the late seventeenth-century and early eighteenth-century sash window frames had usually been painted lead-white, in the later eighteenth century they were painted dark green or – particularly in the early years of the nineteenth century – grained to look like dark oak. In the later nineteenth century, however, the fashion for white-painted sash windows revived, as illustrated in the 1870s work of architects such as Philip Webb and Richard Norman Shaw.

The nineteenth-century fashion for historical styles led to a revival of medieval, Tudor and Elizabethan designs, as well as a serious interest in the making of stained glass. The historicist approach is well illustrated at Scarisbrick Hall in Lancashire in the work of A. W. N. Pugin, who never willingly used sash windows.

OPPOSITE: *The elevation at Farnley Hall, Yorkshire, shows the typical later 18th-century sash window with large rectangular panes of glass. It also illustrates how, in more austere neo-Classical Georgian country houses, windows provided the essential rhythm and relief to a plain façade.*

However, with the development of more effective techniques for producing large plate glass and the repeal of the window tax in 1845 a distinctive Victorian version of the sash emerged, which was made up of only two large panes. The new style was often installed in houses of earlier periods, where the Victorian owner wanted to improve his view out with larger panes. Large single-pane casements were also installed, as, for example, at Waddesdon Manor in Buckinghamshire. By the turn of the century, many country house architects used a variety of casement window types, small-square leaded panes being especially popular with Edwardian architects, including Edwin Lutyens in his early work.

Not all Victorians were fans of the sash, however. French actress Sarah Bernhardt hated the sash, observing: 'English windows only open half way… the sun cannot enter openly and nor the air. The window keeps its selfish and perfidious character. I hate the English window'. She clearly did not understand the mechanics of the sash, as opening the window at the top and the bottom actually increases the air circulation.

RIGHT: *At Middlefield, Cambridgeshire, built in 1910–12 for Cambridge don Dr Henry Bond, the architect Edwin Lutyens combined Georgian-style sash windows with smaller leaded ones, seen on the left.*

LEFT: *Richly decorated and heavy with heraldry, the ornamental chimneypiece at Eastnor Castle in Herefordshire typifies the 19th-century fashion for reviving historical styles.*

CHAPTER TWO

READING THE INSIDE

CHIMNEYPIECES

I<small>N ANY COUNTRY HOUSE</small> one of the elements of the interior that has undoubtedly given principal visual focus to any room has been the chimneypiece. The term chimneypiece is used here to encompass the whole arrangement of fireplace, mantelpiece and any other decorative surround or overmantel. For centuries, the chimneypiece has been so significant and architectural a feature that it can seem almost like a work of architecture in its own right, recalling other characteristically structural features of the country house, an echo of the elaborate frontispieces of the Jacobean era or the Classical porticoes and pediments of the late seventeenth or eighteenth centuries.

A fire in a country house was, until the nineteenth century, the principal source of heat – and therefore of comfort. The architect Isaac Ware, in *The Complete Body of Architecture* (1756), observed that 'with us no article in a well-furnished room is so essential. The eye is immediately cast upon it on entering and the place of sitting down is naturally near it. By this means it becomes the most eminent thing in the finishing of an apartment.'

Even in 1912, the historian L. A. Shuffrey could write 'the open fire certainly remains the most popular, as it is also the most artistic means of heating an apartment; being unequalled not only for its cheerfulness and charm, but also a means of ventilation in constantly changing the air of the room when it is in use'.

NORMAN TO MEDIEVAL: HEARTH AND HOME

IN GREAT HALLS of the Norman and early medieval periods, a fire appears to have normally been placed in a central hearth (or a movable brazier), with smoke escaping through a louvre in the roof, as for example in the great hall of *c*. 1340s at Penshurst in Kent. Soot-blackened timbers, through which the smoke once escaped, can often be seen.

Surviving examples of Norman-style chimneypieces can be seen at Rochester Castle in Kent and Castle Hedingham in Essex. These are set into the castle walls, and are boldly carved with the Norman chevron and semi-circular in shape, in line with the doors and windows of the era.

The other earliest surviving chimneypieces had a pyramidal stone hood, which stood out from the wall and was supported on brackets, as can be seen at the first-floor chamber of the twelfth-century Manor House at Boothby Pagnell, and the fourteenth-century hall at Stokesay Castle in

LEFT: *A boldly detailed, 12th-century Norman-style chimneypiece, built into the main wall at Castle Hedingham, Essex. Note the recurrent chevron (zig-zag) motif, repeated on the window and door arches. At this date, great halls often had central hearths, with the smoke escaping through a hole in the roof.*

Shropshire. Both chimneypieces have a broad hood opening tapering towards a short chimney. The hood type survived until the late fourteenth century, when its broad opening started to recess into the main wall of the hall, as can be seen at the late fifteenth-century Ockwells Manor in Berkshire. Such chimneypieces were usually set in a low arch framed within a square-headed moulding, the space enclosed often finely carved with armorials or quatrefoils, as at Tattershall Castle in Lincolnshire.

RIGHT: *A typically early medieval, projecting, stone hood chimneypiece survives at the Manor House at Boothby Pagnell in Lincolnshire. Supported on stone brackets over a broad hearth, and leading to a low chimney stack, the hood type was a classic medieval form.*

RIGHT: *Early 17th-century Little Castle Bolsover in Derbyshire has an unusually good series of carved stone chimneypieces inlaid with marble. They are based on designs from the Italian treatise* Architettura *(c. 1663), by Sebastiano Serlio.*

ELIZABETHAN TO JACOBEAN: FIRED UP BY ORNAMENT

THE MOST STATELY and enduring decoration of sixteenth- and early seventeenth-century country houses appears on their beautifully modelled chimneypieces and overmantels, which were very much treated as major showpieces, whether in a great country house or humble manor house. The vivid profusion of ornament embellishing the typical Tudor, and especially Elizabethan, chimneypiece would often incorporate Classical ornament on the sides and overmantel, rising up to the ceiling. The Renaissance sources for Classical ornament, such as columns, pilasters and caryatids, were contemporary printed books and engravings, generally imported from Flanders.

A panelled overmantel often included the family's coat of arms, and sometimes the royal arms, or some suitably Protestant-approved Old Testament biblical scene, or possibly a mythological scene, drawn from Classically inspired prints. One favoured Tudor subject for the chimneypiece were the Five Senses, highlighting the pleasures of entertainment on offer at the house.

Some later Elizabethan and early Jacobean chimneypieces in particularly grand houses were often carved in stone and inlaid with coloured marbles in geometric shapes and patterns, such as

LEFT: *The ornamental, 16th-century chimneypiece off the long gallery at Little Moreton Hall, Cheshire, has a characteristically low arch. Note also the decorative heraldic overmantel, typical of chimneypieces built during the later 16th and early 17th centuries.*

RIGHT: *The splendid Palladian chimneypiece at Ditchley Park, Oxfordshire, illustrates the grander type of early 18th-century fireplace. Note how the Palladian detailing on the chimneypiece is mirrored on the interior doorcases.*

at Hardwick Hall, Knole in Kent and the Little Castle Bolsover in Derbyshire, where the design was based on Sebastiano Serlio's *Architettura* (c. 1663).

As wood gave way to coal during the early seventeenth century, the two fire-dogs that had supported large burning logs gave way to a basket-like grate known as dog grates. At the same time, cast-iron firebacks, often decorated with the family coat of arms, became more widespread.

LATER STUART AND GEORGIAN: CLASSICAL COMPOSITIONS

THE GRANDEST EARLY Stuart chimneypieces of the 1630s, such as those at Wilton House in Wiltshire, were based on Classical proportions, drawn from Italian and French precedents. The seventeenth-century diarist John Evelyn praised the work at Wilton as having 'some magnificent chimneypieces after the French best manner'.

Wilton's chimneypieces, however, were at the very top of the scale. In most gentry houses of the Commonwealth and Restoration eras, chimneypieces tended to be bolder and much simpler in form, made in wood, stone or marble (or painted to resemble marble). They are principally notable for taking the typical form of a simple broad, smooth, double curve shape known as a *bolection* moulding. The origin of this charming word is uncertain but it was in use in the seventeenth century.

In the later seventeenth century, the area above the chimneypiece usually matched the form of panelling elsewhere in the room. Sometimes a painting or mirror-glass was set into the panelling above the chimneypiece and flanked by festoons of naturalistic carvings including foliage, fruit and putti (small pudgy Cupids), as at Belton House in Lincolnshire and Petworth House in Sussex.

Something of a fashion for corner chimneypieces arose after the Restoration. Charles II's palace at Newmarket in Suffolk (mostly since demolished) had some – much to the distaste of Evelyn who wrote: '…chimnies in the angles and corners, a mode now introduced by his majesty which I do at no hand approve of. I predict it will spoile many noble houses and rooms if

followed.' Corner examples survive at Hampton Court Palace and at Drayton House in Northamptonshire.

The chimneypieces of the 1720s and 1730s ran more consistently along the model begun by Inigo Jones, as in the work of painter-turned-architect William Kent. In his interiors, the chimneypiece was certainly intended to read as a unified whole. Classical scrolled brackets, often in the form of herms (pillars surmounted with a human bust), supported the mantel. Above the mantel rose a substantial overmantel frame, usually, like so many of the doors of the eighteenth century, capped by a triangular pediment, or by a scrolled (or 'broken') pediment often decorated with a coat of arms.

During the 1720s and 30s the typical overmantel frame usually had corner projections, rather in the manner of ears sticking out (described as 'lugged' or 'lobed', after the ear lobe). The lugged

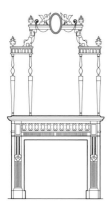

RIGHT: *Typical of the late 18th and early 19th centuries, the fine Classical chimneypiece at Renishaw Hall, Derbyshire, is more restrained in scale and detailing than the earlier and grander varieties of the late 17th and early 18th centuries.*

LEFT: *Late 18th-century Adam-style chimneypieces are noticeably simpler and more refined than earlier 18th-century examples.*

pattern was widely copied, both in town and country, over the early to mid-eighteenth century. Other recurrent motifs included lions' masks and the face of Apollo, the sun god, in a sunburst. In the dining room, Bacchus, the god of wine, commonly appeared, while in the bedrooms, scallop shells alluded to Venus, goddess of love.

As with any popular fashion, something of a reaction followed, producing the lively Rococo style of the 1750s and 1760s. The resultant highly ornamental chimneypieces and overmantel frames, decorated with loosely scrolled, naturalistic shapes, often carved in limewood and gilded, gave visual excitement to the whole chimneypiece and overmantel. Generally rather light and frothy in character, Rococo motifs could be naturalistic, as in the Cabinet Room at Felbrigg Hall in Norfolk, or overtly Oriental, as at Claydon in Buckinghamshire.

Late eighteenth-century Classical interiors, exemplified by Robert Adam, had less over-the-top chimneypieces, more restrained in decoration and often smaller in scale. Typically, such chimneypieces were lighter, with more delicate Classical detailing. Although still incorporating columns or pilasters, Adam's Classical motifs included thin acanthus scrolls, swags of husks, little putti, sphinxes, simplified palmettes, Greek-style altar urns and ox-masks.

Small marble medallions carved in relief were often placed under the centre of the main mantelshelf, sometimes alluding to Bacchus, sometimes to Apollo, or to some other story from the Classical sources. Some of Adam's most handsome chimneypieces were inlaid with coloured marbles rather than carved. Late eighteenth-century grates, usually of polished steel, stood on elegant curved legs, decorated with Classical details reflecting the chimneypiece motifs.

REGENCY TO MODERN: ALIGHT WITH NEW HISTORIES

THE TYPICAL CHIMNEYPIECE of the Regency country house was in some ways plainer still. Often the sides might be grooved to imitate a bundle of reeds, usually with a roundel where the side parts met the upper part. Larger versions were often plain to the point of austerity, but with more monumental elements, such as simple but stout Doric columns.

But the nineteenth-century fashion for building in a variety of Old English styles began in earnest in the same years; chimneypieces would be modelled on medieval and Tudor examples. Throughout the nineteenth century the fact that architects drew on such a wide range of historically based styles meant that no one type of chimneypiece emerged, although it remained a dominant architectural element.

Many architects looked back to the glory days of the 'Mansions of England in Olden Time' as depicted by the artist Joseph Nash in the 1840s. Some harked back to the hood type of the early Middle Ages, as in the splendid work of the Gothic Revival architect, William Burges at Cardiff Castle in Wales.

Others were inspired by the richly carved examples of the later Middle Ages, with its quatrefoils and armorial carving as at Eastnor Castle, Herefordshire. There was also some Classical continuity with the Italianate tradition, as at Queen Victoria and Prince Albert's seaside retreat, Osborne House on the Isle of Wight, and Brodsworth Hall in Yorkshire. The Rothschilds' Waddesdon Manor in Buckinghamshire was inspired by the French court style of King Louis XV.

LEFT: *This remarkable sculptural chimneypiece at Cragside, Northumberland, designed by W. R. Lethaby, effectively creates a small sitting room underneath. Late Victorian taste valued these intimate spaces around a fire.*

READING
THE INSIDE

In late Victorian country houses two types of chimneypiece recur: the inglenook and the display cabinet type. The inglenook fireplace, which encompassed places to sit within the overall structure of the chimneypiece, is something of a feature of the work of the architect R. Norman Shaw, of which the towering marble version at Cragside House in Northumberland, designed by his pupil W. R. Lethaby, is so memorable. Another typical later nineteenth-century form included layers of shelving for the display of fine china above the mantelshelf and sometimes around a mirror, loosely inspired by late seventeenth-century examples.

During the Edwardian era, architects continued to develop various versions of the fireplace, all displaying the skills of that great age of craftsmanship. The varied work of Edwin Lutyens exemplifies the creativity of the era. In his early work, he developed an Arts and Crafts fireplace, reminiscent of the broad hearths of Elizabethan farmhouses, as at Little Thakeham in Sussex; he also experimented with medieval-style wall chimneypieces, as at Castle Drogo in Devon. But in his later work Lutyens tended to favour smooth *bolection*-moulded, late seventeenth-century models.

RIGHT: *Contrived within an alcove and overmantel, Edwin Lutyens' imaginative revival of a late 17th-century bolection-moulded chimneypiece at Heathcote in Yorkshire, is completely Edwardian in character.*

By the early twentieth century Herman Muthesius, the German architectural critic, wrote in *Das Englisch Haus* (1904/5): 'To an Englishman the idea of a room without a fireplace is quite simply unthinkable . . . the fireplace is the domestic altar before which daily and hourly he sacrifices to the household gods.' He also observed: 'Indeed the variety of ways which more recent English art treats these features is inexhaustible.'

Remarkably, despite the sophisticated, computer-aided technology of the twentieth and early twenty-first centuries, the 'open fire' remains a popular feature in many country houses today.

LEFT: *The handsome, late 19th-century chimneypiece at Blackwell, Cumbria, designed by Baillie Scott, combines Arts and Crafts style with the emerging Art Nouveau trend. Blackwell's series of fine chimneypieces were intended to celebrate the harmony of the domestic interior. Baillie Scott himself observed, 'in the house the fire is a substitute for the sun'.*

STAIRCASES

NORMAN TO MEDIEVAL: RISING IN A NARROW COMPASS

THE EARLY STAIRCASES of the Norman and medieval manor house or castle complex were relatively simple affairs. Some early major domestic staircases were external and probably protected by a 'pentice' roof. But the majority of internal staircases tended to be stone and ran either straight up one storey or, more typically, spiralled around a newel, which is literally the pillar, sometimes known as a vice or vyse, around which the steps turn.

Such neat and compact spiral staircases could often be included within the thickness of a wall, set into corner towers or into the angles of towers, and usually, but not always, rose clockwise. Spiral staircases remained the commonest type until the later sixteenth century. Good examples can be seen at Clevedon Court in Somerset or at Belsay Castle in Northumberland. Examples of later medieval brick spiral staircases are found at late fifteenth-century Oxburgh Hall in Norfolk and at Tattershall Castle in Lincolnshire.

ELIZABETHAN TO JACOBEAN: UPWARDS TO GREATER THINGS

THE SELF-CONSCIOUS grandeur of certain Elizabethan country house staircases was a new departure. The steps were wide and rose in short flights, connected by landings – either around a solid rectangular core or around an open well, encircled on the outer edge with a handrail and a balustrade rather than an enclosing wall. In around 1575 Lord Burghley, Elizabeth's Lord Treasurer, installed a remarkable stone staircase at Burghley House that climbs all the way to the roof, modelled on French examples.

When in 1579 Lord Burghley visited fellow courtier Sir Christopher Hatton's house, Holdenby Hall in Northamptonshire, he was struck by the newly built staircase, commenting: 'I found no one thing of greater grace than your stately ascent from your hall to your great chamber.'

LEFT: *The 15th-century stone spiral at Belsay Castle, Northumberland, rising from the great hall to the first floor, is typical of the early medieval staircase, which was, for structural reasons, and perhaps for security, usually a surprisingly narrow affair.*

RIGHT: *The grand Jacobean staircase at Hatfield House, Hertfordshire, abounds with heraldic status symbols. By the late Elizabethan and Jacobean period, the staircase, which had become a major architectural showpiece, leading to the first-floor great chamber, was treated as an opportunity to display pedigree and power.*

An example of an almost processional route to the great high chamber on the first floor can be seen at the remarkable Hardwick Hall. Ascent was still achieved for the most part in relatively short flights, only rising straight up or curving around at the top, on the last few treads, just before reaching the great high chamber. Main staircases in many houses were often sited within stair-towers, as at Montacute in Somerset and Chastleton in Oxfordshire.

The grander Jacobean staircases, like their Elizabethan forerunners, were also usually built around an 'open well', as at Knole in Kent. Handrails were generally very broad and supported by substantial turned balusters or flat slats, which might be either carved or pierced.

Jacobean staircases were often highly decorated, with ornamental motifs carved in the round and often armorial in theme, displaying the family's prestigious pedigree. The characteristic arcading, decoration and pendants seen at Hatfield House in Hertfordshire, with flat balusters

RIGHT: The fine, whitewashed oak staircase at Thorington Hall, Suffolk, one of the smaller 17th-century country houses, is beautifully crafted. Note the carefully detailed newels, balusters and fine pendant decoration, comparable to the grander examples in the local great houses.

and decorated newel posts, are typical of the grander Jacobean staircases, but there were many variations on the theme in smaller country houses as, for example, at Thorington Hall in Suffolk. Sir Henry Wootton observed in his *Elements of Architecture* (1624):

> *To make a compleate staircase is a curious peece of Architecture. The vulgar cautions are these. That it have a very liberall light, aginst all Casualties of slippes, and Falles. That the space above the Head, be large and airy, which the Italians use to call un bel-sfogolo, as it were good Ventilation, because a man doth spend much breather in mounting. That the Halfe-peece bee well distributed, at compenent distances for reposing on the way.*

LATER STUART TO GEORGIAN: STAIRWAY TO HEAVEN

THE LATE STUART staircase is an immediately recognizable type, a grand weighty piece of design and confident craftsmanship, rising up to first-floor reception rooms. A fine example of such elaborate and elegant stairs can be seen at Ham House in Surrey, where the stairs were built as part of improvements made to the house, *c.* 1637–8. A wide and heavily moulded handrail runs above ornate balustrade panelling, with lively carving. In the case of Ham House the carved balustrade panels display trophies of arms, but in many mid- to late seventeenth-century staircases the highly decorated woodwork might be carved with scrolled acanthus leaves instead.

The stout, square newels were usually crowned with carved baskets of fruit and flowers, suggesting plenty. One impressive 1670s example in the same tradition can be seen at Sudbury Hall in Derbyshire with carvings by Edward Pierce. In less grand country houses of the later seventeenth century, staircases would have the same heavily moulded handrails and stout square newels, but the balusters tended to be chunkier and turned (bulbous and vase-shaped).

Many staircases in the grander late seventeenth-century and early eighteenth-century country houses were cantilevered. The technique involved supporting the stairs from the wall by setting

LEFT: *The classic elegance of the early Georgian staircase is clearly illustrated at Frampton Court, Gloucestershire, designed by John Strahan of Bristol in 1731. Note the delicate placement of three finely turned balusters on each step, each running right down to the tread, rather than set in a 'string'.*

each step into the wall, leaving the staircase free of any additional frame beneath, which created an open and airy effect.

The new staircase at Chatsworth was described in 1697 by Celia Fiennes in her diary: 'a fine staircase all of stone and hangs on itself, on the outside, the support is from the wall and its own building, the stone of the half paces are large and one entire stone makes each'.

A more typically early Georgian staircase would probably be in oak with three turned balusters to each tread, supported by a carved bracket underneath. A fine example of this can be seen at Frampton Court in Gloucestershire, where the balusters also stand directly on each tread instead of engaging with a substantial piece of wood, which traditionally ran parallel to the handrail (known as 'the string'). In early to mid-Georgian examples three different styles of turned balusters were often repeated on each tread.

RIGHT: *The archetypal grand Restoration staircase at Thrumpton Hall, Nottinghamshire, has a typically solid, wide baluster rail, with richly carved scrolled acanthus leaves beneath, as well as baskets of fruit on the newel posts. The staircase originally led to state rooms on the first floor.*

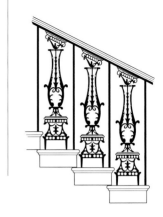

RIGHT: *The late 18th-century staircases of designers such as Robert Adam and James Wyatt are characterized by elegant iron balusters.*

In the mid-eighteenth century staircases continued to make use of the cantilever technology and were often top lit and set in a central staircase hall (some being oval), sometimes with divided upper flights. Mid- to late eighteenth-century stairways also tended to have wrought-iron balusters often with a mahogany handrail. The grandest examples range from such dramatic colonnaded spaces as the main staircase at Wardour Castle in Wiltshire, designed by James Paine, to the more contained geometric examples by Sir Robert Taylor, in houses such as Danson House in Kent.

REGENCY TO MODERN: UPWARD MOBILITY

IN THE REGENCY PERIOD, staircases continued to be objects of great ostentation in country houses, continuing the same play of light and shade initiated in the mid-eighteenth century. Balustrades, still predominantly in ironwork with a polished mahogany handrail, were decorated with balusters. Classical detail, particularly palmettes (stylized palm leaves) were popular.

The grandest late eighteenth-century examples included imperial-style staircases, which rise in the centre and then branch out on either side to glamorous effect, such as those designed by the architect James Wyatt at Heaton Hall in Lancashire. Wyatt also designed the great staircase at Dodington Park in Gloucestershire. Another fine example, Berrington Hall in Herefordshire, designed by Henry Holland, has a handsome colonnaded gallery around the top-lit hall.

In the nineteenth century, the main staircases were principally important as a route to the bedrooms, but they were often combined with the entrance hall to make a show, recapturing the grandeur and dignity of old English examples, as can be found in many great Victorian and

FAR RIGHT: *Scampston Hall, Yorkshire, remodelled around 1800 by Thomas Leverton, has a typically elegant late Georgian/Regency staircase, designed within a relatively confined space, that makes a major architectural statement even though all the reception rooms are on the ground floor.*

Edwardian houses, from Tyntesfield in Somerset to Little Thakeham in Sussex. Secondary staircases, giving servants access to different floors, are also a major element in the nineteenth-century house, part of the careful zoning of country house life at this time.

Main staircases certainly remained part of the pageantry of the country house, setting the stage for many grand entrances, ascents and descents by hostess and house-guests during the many house parties that played such a key part in the life and idea of country houses of the nineteenth and early twentieth centuries.

LEFT: *The splendid neo-Jacobean-style staircase at Stokesay Court, Shropshire, illustrates the ornate decoration characteristic of the grander Victorian house. The massively detailed staircase is so richly decorated with symbols of domestic life that descent to social events must have seemed part of the pageant of country house life.*

PANELLING

BEFORE PANELLING fully developed in the Tudor and particularly in the Elizabethan eras, there seems to have been a very simple oak-board type in the medieval era, with narrow boards placed vertically and either aligned so as to present a smooth surface, or fitted with a narrow rib or fillet to hide the join. Although royal palaces of the early Middle Ages had panelling of some sort, recorded as having been painted green and gilded, none of any note survives. Walls in medieval houses were commonly plastered or painted with decoration. In the grandest houses they might be hung with tapestries or painted cloth.

TUDOR TO JACOBEAN: PANELLED TO PERFECTION

MUCH OF THE MOST attractive panelling likely to be encountered in country houses dates from the Elizabethan and Jacobean periods. William Harrison observed in his *Description of England* (1577):

LEFT: *Panelling became indispensable in the 16th and 17th centuries. This handsome chunky panelling in the great chamber at Haddon Hall, Derbyshire, is said to date from the early 17th century, although the plasterwork is earlier. This sort of panelling was always done in oak with thin panels held in place by a sturdy frame.*

101

RIGHT: *The Tudor great hall at Dorney Court, Berkshire, has a splendid show of linenfold panelling, a ubiquitous element in many 16th-century interiors. Each panel has a rippled effect intended to evoke cloth hangings, the whole creating a happy backdrop to generations of family portraits.*

…the walls of our houses on the inner sides be either hanged with tapestries, arras work or painted cloth, wherein either divers histories, or herbs, beats, knots and such like are stained, or else they are seeled with wood … made more warme and close than otherwise they would be.

By this time many rooms were panelled to dado height and hung with tapestries or painted cloths above. Sir Francis Bacon observed 'musick soundeth better in chambers wainscoted than hanged'. Wainscot is a word used consistently from the sixteenth to the eighteenth century to describe panelling. The Long Gallery at The Vyne in Hampshire has panelling dating from the 1520s.

However, the key advantage offered by panelling was insulation. Another benefit was its decorative possibilities, and in many country houses of the later sixteenth century, the survival of ornately carved or inlaid panelling, combined with rich plasterwork ceilings and carved overmantels, immediately conjures up the Elizabethan period, despite the loss of the original movable furniture and other sources of period colour. Full-height panelling was usually edged with a plasterwork frieze, connecting it to the ceiling above.

ABOVE: *Some fine panelling was, like furniture of the period, enriched with inlay of light coloured woods as in this 1570s example at Sizergh Castle, Cumbria, recently returned to its original setting after a century in the Victoria and Albert Museum, London. The geometric panels below are also typical of Elizabethan and Jacobean panelling.*

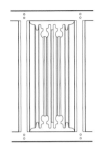

The panelling of the Elizabethan and Jacobean periods was always made from well-seasoned oak, which has since further darkened with age. While sometimes painted, oak panelling seems usually to have been left its own natural plain colour. In essence, panelling of the period was made up of separate thin oak panels, usually around 2ft (60cm) square, held together within a solid timber frame, cut with the necessary grooves into which the boards would fit. The prepared frames and panels would then be joined together by a 'joiner' and pegged in place.

A handsome type of panelling, known as 'linenfold', developed in the Tudor era, early in the sixteenth century. Linenfold panelling, as its name implies, simulates folded cloth. The practice probably arose from the aesthetic enjoyment of handling and looking at lustrous gathered textiles and wall-hangings. Linenfold became the stock panelling for country houses of the sixteenth century. The quality of linenfold varied; the more ornate examples might be decorated with punch holes, suggesting cloth-stitching, while the most simplified versions showed just two simple curves suggesting folds of cloth.

Later sixteenth- and early seventeenth-century panelling was often highly elaborate. The surfaces of the panels and framework were sometimes enlivened with decorative strapwork (derived from cut-leather patterns), or sometimes with other Renaissance Classical motifs, drawn from printed sources, including 'grotesques' based on contemporary excavations of ancient Roman sites.

Sometimes panelling was carved with portrait-style profile busts, clad in contemporary dress and framed in roundels. Alternatively, floral designs might predominate, as at Sizergh Castle in Cumbria, where some fine panelling of the 1570s is inlaid with floral designs highlighted in lighter woods. (The panelling has recently been returned to Sizergh from the Victoria and Albert Museum.)

It is interesting to note that in some later Elizabethan and Jacobean interiors relatively plain overall panelling would be the setting for highly ornamental chimneypiece decoration and doors, as at Montacute in Somerset.

By 1600 panelling was usually divided into geometrical shapes, squares and octagons, and in some rooms a repeated pattern arch and pilaster appears in every panel. Also from about this time,

LEFT: *In 16th-century interiors considerable use was made of linenfold panelling which was intended to resemble folded cloth and to give a lively texture.*

READING
THE INSIDE

tall pilasters (two- rather than three-dimensional columns), running from the floor to the ceiling, were used effectively to divide up rooms visually into bays.

LATER STUART AND EARLY GEORGIAN: KEEPING IT IN PROPORTION

BY THE MID-SEVENTEENTH CENTURY, panelling had changed. It was now formed from much larger panels framed by smoothly rounded and raised joints known as *bolection* moulding, which were usually plain but could carry carving.

This increased scale of panelling was informed by an increased interest in the ideas of Classical architectural proportions. Above the dado, the panels would be tall and vertical, corresponding to a Classical column; below the dado, the panels would be short and horizontal, corresponding to the plinth, or base, of a column. The cornice at ceiling height corresponded to the entablature, which is the horizontal element surmounting the columns of a Classical building.

During the 1660s and early 1670s, panelling appears usually to have been painted. Evelyn wrote of Euston Hall in Suffolk in 1677: 'the wainscot, being of fir and painted, does not please me so well as Spanish oak, without paint'. From the 1680s to the early eighteenth century, natural wood appears to have been favoured, indeed some rooms were expensively panelled in cedar (as at Belton House in Lincolnshire).

The dark wood panelling of the later seventeenth century was often enlivened with applied carving in limewood by, or more usually in the manner of, carver-sculptor Grinling Gibbons, who worked at Hampton Court and at Petworth House in Sussex. These included a familiar range of still-life subjects, as at Belton House, where the carver Mr Carpenter was paid £26 10s for carving 'varieties of fish and sheals/with birds, foliage, fruit & flowers'.

By the early eighteenth century (at the beginning of the Georgian era) most panelling was once again painted if made out of deal (pine or fir). It was in fact usually painted or grained to look like more expensive woods. Early Georgian panelling no longer used bolection moulding. It was usually of a flatter kind known as 'raised and fielded', with the panels raised up to the centre of the frame, but with the edges bevelled back.

RIGHT: *The Classically proportioned panelling at Boughton, Northamptonshire, illustrates the bolection-moulded wainscot during the late 17th and early 18th centuries. Modelled on the proportions of the Classical column, the panel below the dado rail corresponds with the base of the column, the tall middle panel with the column's shaft, and the upper panel with the column's capital. Note also the bolection-moulded chimneypiece.*

By the mid-eighteenth century, plaster became the preferred surface for walls, as it was regarded as more Classical in spirit, more reflective of light and more effective as a fire-precaution. Chair or dado rails were often still carved in wood, while the panels below were now more likely to be rendered in plaster. Wallpaper also became increasingly popular in the later eighteenth century, particularly from the 1770s onwards.

In Regency interiors, fully panelled rooms in the Classical manner were rare, as paints and wallpapers offered popular decorative solutions in the various tributaries of the neo-Classical style, such as Egyptian and Greek revivals. However, the early nineteenth century did see a great enthusiasm for recreating the atmosphere of the Elizabethan and Jacobean manor house interiors, in which stout oak panelling had played such an impressive part. Few country houses reached the dizzying richness of Scarisbrick Hall in Lancashire, where Pugin incorporated authentic antique carving; but, elsewhere, oak panelling was widely revived for use in country house decoration.

Although some simple tongue-and-groove panelling was used, most Victorian panelling imitated the Elizabethan and Jacobean types. Certain rooms, such as entrance halls, libraries and billiard rooms, were usually fully panelled, but other spaces were often only panelled to dado or chair rail height, combined with richly patterned wallpapers.

From the 1870s, the Queen Anne Revival saw a fashion for white painted panelling and renewed interest in the larger panels of the later seventeenth century. Natural wood colour became popular, but panelling could be painted white or occasionally green, particularly around 1900.

Some adherents of the Arts and Crafts philosophy espoused by William Morris aimed to recreate panelling by the same hand-crafted methods as were used originally, as can be seen in the early twentieth-century work of Ernest Gimson and Sidney Barnsley at Rodmarton Manor in Gloucestershire. At the other end of the scale there was a vogue for buying old panelling, or making new panelling and distressing it to appear old, giving a slightly 'pickled' look.

Other early twentieth-century architects and designers imitated Elizabethan and Jacobean panelling, as can be seen in the work of Edwin Lutyens at Munstead Wood in Surrey and Deanery Gardens, Berkshire.

In 1904, Herman Muthesius observed:

> ...wood panelled walls are more popular in England than almost any other country. This was already true of old houses ... It is almost as if the inmates looked to this warm, comfortable interior motif, to compensate for inhospitable nature outside.

It is interesting to note wood was used in many Modernist houses, but usually plain plywood and never panelled, such as the interiors of Erno Goldfinger's No. 1 Willow Road in Hampstead.

LEFT: *A popular finish in 19th-century Revivalist interiors, panelling helped to recreate the much-admired, warm, well-insulated effect of 16th- and 17th-century country houses. Revivalist styles ranged from the full-blooded Gothic of A. W. N. Pugin at Scarisbrick Hall, Lancashire, to the domestic interiors of Edwin Lutyens, as shown here, at Deanery Gardens, Berkshire, designed in 1899.*

PLASTERWORK CEILINGS

TUDOR TO JACOBEAN: PRETTY AND PREPOSTEROUS

ALTHOUGH PLASTER, a lime-based render, had been used for centuries to finish off and insulate the internal walls of houses, the really distinctive decorative use of plasterwork on country house ceilings developed in the sixteenth century, enduring, in varying and different forms, until the twentieth century. Two important early patrons who helped develop plasterwork were Henry VIII (at Nonesuch Palace in Surrey) and Cardinal Wolsey (at Hampton Court). And where the king led, court and country followed.

RIGHT: *The ribs of the plasterwork ceiling at Lytes Cary in Somerset emulate the pattern of the stone-vaulted ceilings of the later Middle Ages. Such plasterwork was usually carried out using running moulds.*

LEFT: *The splendid plaster chimneypiece at Charlton House in Greenwich illustrates the rich, layered type of plasterwork characteristic of the very early 17th century, with figures in relief and strapwork, derived from cut leather patterns. Plaster ceilings of the period tended to be decorated with geometric patterns and bold pendant details.*

RIGHT: *Ornate ceiling panels in the early 17th-century great chamber at Speke Hall, Lancashire, richly decorated with intertwined vine leaves. As the principal room for entertaining honoured guests, the great chamber tended to be the most lavishly decorated.*

It is worth remembering that plasterwork, panelling and chimneypieces are the surviving fixtures, which would have been matched in vibrancy and detail by the movable furnishings. The ceilings of the sixteenth-century country house were usually decorated with an interlaced pattern or ribs in low relief plasterwork. The ribs that typify Tudor work (as in the great chamber of Lytes Cary Manor in Somerset) seem to have originated from the pattern of ribs in the stone vaulting of medieval ceilings.

Plaster was commonly worked *in situ* by pressing moulds into wet plaster, or using running tools to create continuous ornament. The compartments created by the plasterwork were often picked out with heraldic details or with stylized floral devices, birds and animals, which would have held significance for the Tudor observer.

Popular themes were commonly drawn from printed sources such as Geoffrey Whitney's *A Choice of Emblems* (1586) and Henry Peacham's *Minerva Britannia* (1612), or the motifs produced by Wendel Dietterlein and Vriedeman de Vries. The contemporary advances in

printing that had led to wide circulation of printed pattern sources in turn helped transform the imaginative world of both craftsman and patron.

Plasterers were much sought after as highly skilled craftsmen who could greatly contribute to the decoration of country houses, as can be seen in Sir William Cavendish's letter to Sir John Thynne at Longleat: 'I understand that you have a connyng plaisterere at Longlete who haith in your hall and in your other places of your house mad[e] diverse pendants and other prettye thynges.' (Pendants are the attractively formed plaster pieces that hang down from the ceiling at the point where the ribs meet.)

A grand Tudor plasterwork frieze survives in Hardwick Hall's great high chamber, *c.* 1590s. Although the chamber's ceilings are fairly plain, its walls are dominated by a large plasterwork frieze, created by Abraham Smith and others. Originally painted in vivid colour, it depicts Diana and her court, probably by way of compliment to Queen Elizabeth. The scenes in the great high chamber were based on Flemish engravings by the master engravers Cornelius de Vos and

Nicholaes de Bruyn. It is thought likely that, originally, more plasterwork would have been picked out in colour, especially around chimneypieces.

LATER STUART TO GEORGIAN: CLASSICAL CACOPHONY

IN CONTRAST TO Jacobean ceilings, Stuart plasterwork of the later seventeenth century was compartmented into a smaller number of panels. Typically, grand ceilings of the period were designed with a large central circle or oval, surrounded by a border, cornice and frieze, harking back to the early Palladian designs of Inigo Jones in the 1630s.

The ceiling patterns, inspired by Italian Renaissance examples, provided square and oblong spaces for paintings, which were very richly ornamented in high relief with naturalistic foliage, swags of fruit and flowers that served almost as three-dimensional still lives, as can be seen at the Banqueting House at Whitehall. Ceilings in high relief, however, were more characteristic of the

LEFT: *This ceiling detail at Coleshill, Berkshire (sadly demolished) illustrates the influence of Andrea Palladio during the 17th century, via the work of Inigo Jones, leading to a plainer design of broadly geometric patterns, including large ovals intended for paintings. At this period the ribs were decorated almost in the manner of still-life paintings.*

later seventeenth century. Sir Roger North, the amateur architect, wrote in 1660: '…in the several divisions let the panels be raised about half an inch, or a whole one, and bordered with some lace, eggs and ancors etc, and the void filled with cornucopias, Mercuries, ensigns, crowns of laurel or oak'.

A splendid example of this kind of work can be found in the staircase hall and the saloon of Sudbury Hall in Derbyshire, executed by Robert Bradbury and James Pettifer for George Vernon. The scrolls and swags, the palms and the scallop shells are modelled with extraordinary depth and vivacity, creating a kind of three-dimensional still life that literally hangs from the ceiling. The major rooms in numerous less grand manor houses showed a more restrained version of these basic patterns.

Early Georgian plasterwork, in the houses associated with the country houses of the Palladian movement, is sometimes more carefully modelled on Roman examples, such as the heavy gilded, coffered ceiling at Lord Burlington's Chiswick House. However, the great novelty of the 1720s was the work of the renowned Italian plasterers, known as the stuccadores, after the stucco plaster in which they worked. The stuccadores, who created some of the most breathtaking interior decoration in Britain, first seem to have been employed at Ditchley Park in Oxfordshire and Castle Howard in Yorkshire.

The stuccadores, also known as 'fretworkers', who came mostly from the Ticino region, now part of Switzerland, brought with them Continental Baroque decoration, sophisticated fretwork and Classical figurework. The stuccadores were masters of the human form and excelled in Classical history and mythological scenes, peopled with legendary Caesars, deities and heroes, such as Venus and Adonis, Diana and Actaeon. Most of the scenes were drawn from contemporary printed sources such as the *Iconologia* (1593) of Cesare Ripa.

The stuccadores' fine stucco plaster was further refined with added marble dust and modelled *in situ*. The earliest example of the stuccadores' work appears to have been by Plura and Giovanni Bagutti, who designed the decoration over the chimneypiece in the great hall at Castle Howard in the first decade of the eighteenth century. In the following decades the great stuccadores were

LEFT: Hagley Hall, Worcestershire, contains much good plasterwork of the mid-18th century with mythological figures framed in panels, and busts of Roman emperors set on brackets.

RIGHT: The Classically inspired ceilings at Syon Park, Middlesex, designed by Robert Adam, were informed by new examples of Greco-Roman decoration emerging from 18th-century archaeological excavations. The delicate fine swags of 'husks' are a very characteristic motif of this era.

the Artari brothers, who worked at Ditchley Park; and La Francini who worked at Wallington Hall in Northumberland. The fashion for stucco plasterwork in country house interiors continued well into the 1750s, of which fine examples are Honington Hall in Warwickshire and Easton Neston in Northamptonshire, where mythological scenes are depicted in elegant handsome plaster frames.

Certain English regional families of plasterers dominated the rest of the scene, often collaborating with the stuccadores who would specialize in the figure work. Thomas Clark worked on the hugely impressive Classical Roman-style entrance hall at Holkham Hall in Norfolk. More modest late seventeenth-century and early eighteenth-century interiors would have simpler cornices of carved or plain repeated blocks, known as 'modillion'.

Later eighteenth-century Georgian plaster decoration, in the neo-Classical manner, was generally much lighter in effect, as can be seen in the work of Sir William Chambers and Robert

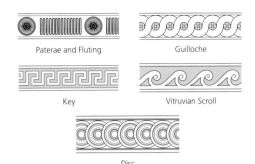

Paterae and Fluting

Guilloche

Key

Vitruvian Scroll

Disc

LEFT: *Typical Georgian plasterwork details.*

RIGHT: *The grander Victorian country house made happy use of historical precedents in recreating handsome Tudorbethan ceilings, as for instance here in the drawing room of Stokesay Court, Shropshire. As Victorian plasterwork was, however, cast in moulds rather than modelled in situ, it rarely captured the hand-modelled qualities of 16th- or 17th-century plasterwork.*

Adam, characterized by swags of husks and roundels. The decorative ceilings of this era became more one-dimensional, consisting of repeated patterns spread across the whole room, ceiling and walls. This type of work was mostly executed in moulds and no longer modelled *in situ*.

Adam introduced a new vocabulary of detail, including a delicate type of grotesque, inspired by Classical Roman and Italian Renaissance decoration. Later Georgian cornices tended to be designed with simpler enrichments, such as urns, rosettes and a pleated tent motif, associated with the work of Adam and James Wyatt.

Ceiling patterns of the period were often composed in a series of interconnecting curves, combined with painted colour schemes, with gilding and applied canvas roundels, depicting figures from Classical mythology, as can be seen at Osterley Park and Syon House, both in Middlesex.

In the Georgian era there were many plaster ceilings in the Gothic manner, as for example at Strawberry Hill in Twickenham, a precursor to many Gothic Revival and Elizabethan-style ceilings of the nineteenth century. In the long gallery at Strawberry Hill, the Gothic-style plasterwork was modelled on the fan vaulting of the Henry VII chapel at Westminster Cathedral, which became a key model for the eighteenth-century Gothic Revival.

REGENCY TO MODERN: PLASTERING WITH PURPOSE

SOME REGENCY PLASTERWORK ceilings are sumptuous in the extreme, as for instance the Chinese style fish-scale plaster decoration at the Brighton Pavilion (designed by John Nash for the Prince Regent) and the gilded French Rococo-style plasterwork by Francis Bernasconi at Belvoir Castle in Rutland. There were a number of Gothic extravagances, but in the more sober neo-Classical country houses plaster decoration was more restrained.

The neo-Classical taste of the early nineteenth century looked not to the extreme delicacy developed by Adam, but rather to a more robust and severe style, associated with the work of John Soane, recalling what was then perceived as the weight and austerity of early Classical, particularly Greek, architecture. In most instances, however, Regency plasterwork ceilings were

more restrained, simpler in detail and bolder in effect, with decoration confined to centrepieces and cornices.

The plasterwork ceilings of the later nineteenth century were modelled in great and varied quantity on the glories of old English plasterwork, but tended to be cast rather than modelled *in situ*, achieving a more precise line than their sixteenth- and seventeenth-century predecessors. Late nineteenth- and early twentieth-century followers of the Arts and Crafts philosophy of hand craftsmanship tried to revive the handmodelling of plaster *in situ*. One principal practitioner, George Bankart, worked in the style of late seventeenth-century plasterwork. Another, Ernest Gimson, based in the Cotswolds, imitated the texture and quality of early Tudor work.

Later twentieth-century decorative plasterwork is rare, although there have been some major restorations and reconstructions, including the ceilings of Uppark in Petersfield. Rococo-style plasterwork was created for Gervase Jackson Stops by the artist Christopher Hobbs for The Menagerie in Northamptonshire, featuring the music from *Animal Crackers in My Soup*.

·TK· ·W·

·THINKE and THANKE·
⋮ 1897 ⋮

LEFT: *A glass roundel at Davington Priory, Kent, designed by Thomas Willement, a pioneer of the early 19th-century revival of heraldry, an essential tool of display, celebrates Willement's own status and connections as owner of Davington.*

CHAPTER THREE

READING THE SYMBOLS

Heraldry in the Country House

ERALDRY IS UNDOUBTEDLY one of the greatest sources of imagery used in the interior and exterior decoration of an English country house. For instance, when Knole in Kent was rebuilt in 1603, Thomas Sackville, the 1st Earl of Dorset, incorporated heraldic imagery everywhere, on the outside and inside, from the carved stone spotted leopard of Sackville clasping the Sackville arms, to the heraldic details decorating the ornate screen in the great hall carved by William Portington, master carpenter to Elizabeth I and James I. The heraldic theme continues on Knole's great staircase, where the Sackville arms appear both in wood and stained glass.

Heraldry has always been, in essence, a form of codified display of aristocratic status, and also became an important way of illustrating family alliances. On the Knole screen, for instance, the arms of Sackville appear 'impaled' (or combined) with the arms of his wife's family, Baker of Sissinghurst, showing that she also came from a family of high status.

Heraldry itself is most simply described as the hereditary use of symbols, technically known as 'charges' or 'devices' on a shield, although it developed into a complex set of laws. In brief, a full

coat of arms, known as 'an achievement', will also include a crest (the display on top of a helmet, known as a 'helm'); supporters (the figures bearing the shield, of which the best known are the lion and unicorn on the royal coat of arms); coronets and badges denoting noble rank; and mottoes.

It used to be thought that heraldry began in the twelfth century as a way of identifying different individuals in battle. However, heraldry is now thought to have been more a product of the highly ritualized world of pageantry and tournaments practised by the knightly class. Although associated with warfare and chivalry, heraldry probably was not actually developed for battle-wear.

The critical moment when heraldry entered English interior decoration has been traced to a visit made by Henry III to Paris in 1254, when he was greatly impressed by the decoration used at a banquet given by Louis IX. Louis had hung the banqueting hall with painted shields of the arms of the noble houses of France, as if for a tournament.

When Henry III returned to London he copied the idea in the carved stone decoration of Westminster Abbey, with brightly painted shields of the royal family and principal barons. The

LEFT: *The great hall screen at Knole in Kent was richly carved by the royal carpenter William Portington for Thomas, Earl of Sackville. It is simply loaded with heraldic ornament, including the Sackville leopards on either side of the base of the doorcase, and shields or arms above. Coronets crowning a shield indicate a titled rank.*

decoration was soon copied in other royal cathedrals and palaces, and then in the castles of the king's barons.

Many shields were originally designed with simple stripes and crosses and a small range of bold colours. However, the practice, which originated in Spain, of quartering arms to show dynastic marriages with other arms-bearing families became popular in England after the marriage of Henry III's son Edward I to Eleanor of Castile.

From the late thirteenth century, and perhaps reaching an apogee in the sixteenth and early seventeenth centuries, heraldry thus provided excellent (and non-religious) motifs for the woodcarvers and sculptors, stained glass artists and plasterers employed to beautify a country house. The many shields carved on the early fifteenth-century chimneypiece in the Great Chamber at Tattershall Castle in Lincolnshire are eloquent statements of the status and network of its founder, Ralph, Lord Cromwell, who had fought at Agincourt in 1415 and was Lord High Treasurer of England from 1433 to 1443.

RIGHT: *On the handsomely carved stone chimneypiece in the parlour at Tattershall Castle, Lincolnshire, an array of heraldic emblems display family status and connections. The recurrent armorial motif of a purse celebrates the high office attained by Ralph Lord Cromwell, who served as Lord High Treasurer from 1433 to 1443.*

LEFT: *The arms of Bess of Hardwick, depicted in pole position over the chimney-piece of the great hall at Hardwick Hall, Derbyshire. Handsomely carved in relief in the 1590s, the arms are framed by two stag 'supporters' with real antlers. Heraldic decoration embellished entrances, great halls, and great chambers and was an essential part of outward display.*

Heraldry clearly celebrated both genealogy and connections. King James I, on seeing the heraldic and genealogical decoration at Lumley Castle, is said to have remarked, 'I didna ken that Adam's name was Lumley.'

An elaborate coat of arms was often found above the entrance to a house, as seen over the gatehouse to fifteenth-century Herstmonceux Castle in Sussex and early sixteenth-century East Barsham Manor in Norfolk. A coat of arms could also appear in a number of different places in a great hall: at the dais end, as in the great hall at Raglan Castle in Wales; in stained glass, as at Rufford Old Hall in Lancashire; or above a principal chimneypiece, as in Hardwick Hall. Another typical place for heraldry was over the chimneypiece in the great chamber, as in Little Moreton Hall in Cheshire. Sometimes in a great chamber one also finds the royal coat of arms, often underlining allegiance to a monarch, as at Hardwick Hall.

A coat of arms also often appears as a dominant element in a plaster ceiling decoration, as in the 1590s great parlour at Broughton Castle in Oxfordshire or the long gallery (now library) at Blickling Hall in Norfolk. From the sixteenth century onwards, crests were also widely used as decorative motifs in their own right.

Initially, it seems that coats of arms were self-assumed, but the bearing of a coat of arms was always closely identified with gentle birth or high rank. From the fifteenth century onwards, the granting of arms fell under ever more stringent royal control. Richard III formed the College of Arms, consisting of officials called Kings of Arms, heralds and pursuivants. The College of Arms could oversee English heraldry and genealogy, but more importantly police

BELOW: *The Jacobean screen in the great hall at
Bramshill House, Hampshire, groans with painted
shields proclaiming the family connections of Lord
Zouch, the builder of Bramshill. Heraldic decoration, the
first major non-religious source of images used in country
house decoration, remains a persistent feature to this day.*

and control the use of arms by 'visitations' or tours of the provinces to record the coats of arms
in current use.

The granting of new arms was delegated by the sovereign to the Kings of Arms under the
supervision of the Earl Marshal. Grants of arms were regularly made to newly empowered men
who used their wealth to establish landed dynasties and display their new social status with
recurrent heraldic decoration.

RIGHT: *The Brownlows' coat of arms at Belton House,
Lincolnshire, is carved within a cartouche (scrolled
Classical frame) on the main pediment. Although by this
time, heraldic detail was not as overpowering as in the 17th
century, the resonance of family status was just as vital.*

In the seventeenth century, the rise of Classical taste led to a more restrained style of heraldry, typically restricted to a cartouche in the main pediment, as at Belton House in Lincolnshire, or to a simplified crest and date, or perhaps coronets carved on the lead heads of rainwater down-pipes. With the increasing influence of the more austere Palladian school of architecture and later neo-Classical taste, heraldry gradually ceased to feature so prominently in exterior architecture.

HERALDRY ON A PLATE

HERALDRY IS SO TIED UP with upper-class identity, however, that it somehow developed into a yet more intimate feature of country house life. Heraldic decoration remains a regular feature within the entrance hall, on the backs of hall chairs (facing the onlooker from the front) and on servants' livery, for instance, the depiction of the crest on silver buttons. Personalized bookplates pasted in the front of books in the library for identification might also display the family crest, along with writing paper. This type of low-key, intimate heraldry has sometimes been referred to as 'buttonmakers' heraldry'. Finely painted coats of arms also appeared on the doors of coaches.

Most major country houses also have examples of heraldic display on silver and porcelain, associated with the prestige of the dining room and table. On silver, heraldic display might include a full coat of arms, or simply a crest engraved on a dish or tureen. Sometimes, the crest might take the form of a handle, as in the case of the Frederick Kandler tureen at Ickworth in Suffolk, on which the Hervey family crest forms the crowning handle.

In the eighteenth century, it became the fashion among British patrons to order Chinese porcelain services from Chinese manufacturers. The services would be decorated with heraldic devices, reproduced from a sketch or bookplate. One fine example at Hanbury Hall in Worcestershire shows a dinner service decorated with the crest of the Vernon family (typically a woman with a wheatsheaf), transformed by a Chinese artist into a Chinaman with a rice sheaf.

The traditions of heraldry were challenged in the early nineteenth century by requests for pictorial representations of historical events, such as the naval battle scenes shown on Lord

RIGHT: *Highclere Castle, Hampshire, was embellished in the 1860s with handsome interiors by Thomas Allom, in which coats of arms played an important part.*

LEFT: *The English aristocracy of the later 18th century rarely missed a chance to decorate their table china or silver with family crests, as seen on this silver plate from Kedleston Hall, Derbyshire, etched with the arms of the 1st Lord Scarsdale.*

Nelson's arms. At the same time, renewed interest in heraldry arose alongside the Gothic Revival of the late eighteenth and early nineteenth centuries, notably in the work of A. W. N. Pugin and Thomas Willement, heraldic artist to King George IV.

Pugin's rigorous attention to the traditions of heraldic decoration occurs throughout the new Palace of Westminster, clearly visible on the throne on which Elizabeth II sits for the annual state opening of Parliament. Pugin's decoration at Westminster includes the repeated use of the Beaufort armorial badge of a 'portcullis', still perhaps one of the most immediately recognizable images associated with the British government today.

HERALDRY REVIVED: A CALL TO ARMS

THE REVIVAL OF INTEREST in heraldry in the early nineteenth century was also associated with nationalistic pride in the overthrow of Napoleon at the battle of Waterloo in 1815 after a long war. Heraldic decoration came to be as liberally used throughout country houses as it had been in the sixteenth century. Fine examples survive in the State Drawing Room of the novelist Bulwer Lytton at Knebworth House in Hertfordshire; and in Pugin's work for Charles Scarisbrick at Scarisbrick Hall in Lancashire, or for the Earl of Shrewsbury at Carlton Towers in Yorkshire; also in Thomas Allom's designs at Highclere Castle in Berkshire for the 4th Earl of Carnavon.

The revival and restoration of old glass in the great halls of country houses was a popular pastime throughout the nineteenth century. Older glass was bought up to make up losses, providing a delightful source of family and antiquarian pride, while also creating a fine dappled light effect in the interior.

Heraldic ornament continued to be used in the early twentieth century, examples being the great crest carved over the entrance to Castle Drogo in Devon or the display of coronets on the 1920s estate cottages built by the 2nd Lord Fairhaven at Anglesey Abbey. Heraldry has in more recent times been associated with church monuments. Grants of new coats of arms continue to be made to the present day, which illustrates something of the extraordinary adaptability of heraldry as an enduring system of imparting a permanent record (in colour and line) of individual achievement.

LEFT: *Christian symbols abound at Burton Agnes Hall in Yorkshire. A great screen depicts the 12 sons of Jacob, with scenes from their life, and the figures of Peace and Concord. Above the screen runs a plaster frieze showing the Four Evangelists and the Apostles. On the grand chimneypiece, female figures represent the Five Senses and the parable of the Wise and Foolish Virgins.*

Christian Symbols
in the Country House

JUSTICE AND SALVATION

THE GREAT MEDIEVAL royal and aristocratic interiors were apparently decorated with tapestries and wall paintings, now lost, illustrating the key stories of the Bible. The thirteenth-century painted chamber in the Palace of Westminster, for instance, once had depictions of the Miracles of Elisha, the story of Hezekiah, St Edward with a pilgrim and Edward the Confessor. A fine fourteenth-century painted interior that does survive in Longthorpe Tower in Cambridgeshire shows the Nativity, the Seven Ages of Man, St Anthony the Hermit, the Four Evangelists and King David. A late fourteenth-century depiction of the Virgin Mary and child also survives at Cothay Manor, in Somerset.

However, the break with the Roman Catholic Church in the early sixteenth century saw a Protestant rejection of traditional images of the Virgin and saints, the use of which was regarded as idolatrous. During the later sixteenth and early seventeenth centuries, such scriptural subjects were usually avoided, although certain biblical stories from the Old Testament and Apocrypha do emerge in decorative schemes in the later sixteenth and early seventeenth centuries, particularly in overmantels, carved in wood or modelled in plaster.

At Burton Agnes in Yorkshire, for instance, the great hall screen has the Twelve Tribes of Israel and the overmantel the parable of the Wise and Foolish Virgins; at Apethorpe Hall in Northamptonshire, King David is shown playing the harp. In the long gallery at Hardwick Hall, the alabaster figures of Justice and Mercy have long been thought to show where Bess of Hardwick sat as magistrate over her tenants and household. Carved figures of Hope, Justice, Faith and Mercy can, indeed, be found in many houses, including Wolfeton House in Dorset.

In similar vein, several overmantels depict biblical stories rarely shown in churches but possibly related to civic judgement (the role of the local magistrate). An example is the story of

Susannah and the Elders, as seen at Chillingham Castle. While innocently bathing in her garden, Susannah is propositioned by two elders; when she refuses their advances they denounce her, but Daniel proves their testimony false through a wise and thorough examination.

Another recurrent story is that of the Sacrifice of Isaac, a moral admonishing spiritual obedience and perhaps illustrating divine mercy. Isaac proved his obedience when he followed a divine order to sacrifice his son, who was reprieved at the last moment. At Stockton House in Wiltshire the Shadrach Room shows the Three Youths in the Fiery Furnace, from the Book of Daniel. Curiously enough, of course, they were cast into the fiery furnace for refusing to bow down to an idol, but rescued by divine intervention, perhaps demonstrating God's protection of the innocent or righteous.

Despite the decline of biblical imagery in the country house interior from the early 1600s, the chapel remained an important feature of the country house. In any medieval household of status the private chapel was a necessary part of the private household. The Roman Catholic chapel at Stonor Park in Oxfordshire dates back at least to 1331. Another good example of a fourteenth-century private chapel can be found at Broughton Castle in Oxfordshire.

How central the chapel remained in the mind of an Elizabethan is shown in Sir Francis Bacon's *On Building* (1597), where he described his ideal palace: 'on the household side, I wish it divided at the first into a Hall and Chappell (with a Partition betweene both of good State and Bignesse)'. Two excellent examples of little-altered, early seventeenth-century chapels can be seen at Knole in Kent, where the original fifteenth-century chapel was refitted for the Sackvilles; and at Hatfield House's chapel in Hertfordshire, built for Robert Cecil, 1st Earl of Salisbury, where, remarkably, daily morning prayer is still heard.

A HOUSEHOLD AT PRAYER

IN THE GRANDER late seventeenth-century country house, the family chapel would often be contrived to fill one of the wings, as at Belton House in Lincolnshire. Belton has an ornate Classical reredos with paired columns supporting a pediment that seems remarkable for a

RIGHT: *In the immensely elegant, two-storey chapel at 1680s Belton House, Lincolnshire, the family pew looked down from the gallery onto the remarkable, marble Classical reredos, shown here. Note the Grinling Gibbons linenwood carving at centre.*

Protestant chapel, but was in line with the taste expressed in Wren's city churches. The household would be seated at ground level in box-pews, while the family was accommodated in a private gallery pew, with velvet upholstery and a fire to warm them.

Eighteenth-century chapels are found only in the very largest houses, such as Holkham Hall in Norfolk, and Wimpole Hall in Cambridgeshire, where the handsome chapel was painted for Lord Harley by James Thornhill. The chapel, muralled with the Adoration of the Magi, was possibly intended as much for the performance of choral music.

Such eighteenth-century chapels illustrate a softening of attitude towards religious imagery by this date, partly influenced by art historical connoisseurship of the Old Master painters among the aristocracy, who sometimes presented religious paintings to local churches. For most landowners, however, the family pew in the local parish church was treated effectively as a chapel for their family, who in many cases had the right to appoint the vicar to his 'living'.

Towards the end of the eighteenth century Lord Arundel of Wardour developed a handsome Catholic chapel at Wardour Castle in Wiltshire, designed by James Paine. A great lofty colonnaded space filled with Italian paintings of the saints, it is used today as a Catholic church.

LEFT: *The elegant 1860s High Victorian chapel at Tyntesfield, Somerset, designed by Sir Arthur Blomfield, is rich with medieval Christian imagery. Said to be one of the largest private chapels in England, Tyntesfield illustrates the High Church revival.*

The Gothic Revival in architecture of the nineteenth century was closely tied up with a wider religious revival, and a huge number of parish churches were restored or built in styles reflecting the best of medieval precedents, and emphasizing a return to a sacramental tradition, with a high altar. It is interesting to note that the use of candles and crosses, vestments and choirs that we take for granted in the twenty-first century was part of a nineteenth-century revival.

A number of new country house chapels were built in the Gothic Revival style, of which one of the finest is a cathedral-like chapel created for the Duke of Newcastle to designs by G. F. Bodley at Clumber Park (the house now demolished) in Nottinghamshire. Another example is the handsome 1870s chapel at Tyntesfield in Somerset, designed by Arthur Blomfield. Examples of early twentieth-century chapels can be found at Rodmarton Manor in Oxfordshire and Berkeley Castle in Gloucestershire. Perhaps the most recent example of a new chapel is that at Deene Park in Northamptonshire.

Anyone visiting a country house today would, of course, do well to look at the local parish church and inspect the major monuments in sculpted marble, which tell us such a lot about the lives (and deaths) and ambitions of the landowning class.

National History in the Country House

Courage, loyalty and liberty

In sixteenth-century decoration, legendary heroes of Romantic English history do occasionally appear. One great British hero is King Arthur. He does not make his appearance alone, however, but usually as part of a team of Worthies, the Nine Worthies to be precise, as the poet John Henry Dryden recalled in his poem 'The Flower and the Leaf' in *Fables* (1700), supposedly based on a tale by Chaucer:

> *Nine Worthies were they called, of different rites*
> *Three Jews, three pagans and three Christian Knights.*
> *These, as you see, ride foremost in the field,*
> *As they the foremost rank of honour held*
> *And all in deeds of chivalry excell'd*

The Worthies are Joshua, David and Judas Maccabeus (Jews), Hector, Alexander and Caesar (pagans) and Arthur, the Emperor Charlemagne and Godfrey of Bouillon, who led the first crusade and became the first Christian king of Jerusalem. Each Worthy exemplified knightly chivalric virtues; Arthur, for instance, allegedly brought order, unity and prosperity to the English kingdom, and represented a heroic ideal for the English knight. In Shakespeare's *Love's*

RIGHT: *In the Temple of Saxon Worthies, erected by Viscount Cobham at Stowe, Buckinghamshire, in 1735, national heroes are celebrated in sculpture by Jan Michiel Rysbrack and Peter Scheemakers. Among the popular worthies are the writers Shakespeare and Milton, and the monarchs Elizabeth I and William II, regarded as having preserved political liberty.*

RIGHT: *Busts of Roman emperors collected by William Holbeck while on his Grand Tour fill the hall at Farnborough Hall, Warwickshire. Holbeck also brought together an important collection of paintings.*

Labour's Lost, the comic characters attempt to stage a masque based on the Nine Worthies, and famously make a great hash of it. The Nine Worthies can be found on the main front of late sixteenth-century Montacute in Somerset and in the courtyard of Chillingham Castle in Northumberland.

One of the main early eighteenth-century examples of national heroes appears in the amazing Elysian Fields of Stowe. Its owner, Lord Cobham, a prominent politician of the progressive Whig party, created a temple to commemorate the historical Britons he most admired. Cobham commissioned 16 busts by leading sculptors Jan Michiel Rysbrack and Peter Scheemakers, which were set into a temple designed by William Kent, and reflected in the lake.

The heroes include, on one side, men of arts and letters: the poet Alexander Pope; Sir Thomas Gresham, founder of the Royal Exchange; the architect Inigo Jones; the poet John Milton; the playwright William Shakespeare; the philosopher John Locke; the scientist Isaac Newton; the writer and scientist Francis Bacon. On the other side appear those whose lives contributed to British liberty, through arms and statecraft: the Black Prince; King Alfred; Queen Elizabeth I; King William II; the explorers Sir Walter Raleigh and Sir Francis Drake; the MP John Hampden; the economist Sir John Barnard. The men of arts and letters also appear in other country houses, often in sets of busts designed for the library, where their books would be read.

MARKING TRIUMPHS

ANOTHER FEATURE of national history reflected in the country house and its park is the evocation of the battlefield. At Blenheim Palace in Oxfordshire, the tree plantings apparently represent the battle formations of the Duke of Marlborough's great triumph at Blindheim in 1706. Certainly the Triumphal Arch and Column of Victory at Blenheim refer directly to his martial exploits. In another example, the eighteenth-century gentleman architect Sanderson Miller built a castle on his estate in Warwickshire where he believed Charles I had raised his standard at the battle of Edgehill; Miller also planted the area with trees to represent the regiments that were involved in the battle.

Classical Mythology in the Country House

The happy triumphs of love and learning

WHETHER IN PLASTER, paint or wood, almost every face, figure, plant and animal depicted in the country houses of the seventeenth and eighteenth centuries originated in the myths and legends of Classical Greece and Rome. The brief survey mapped out here, covering the most frequently encountered Classical themes and scenes, should provide a useful key to reading seventeenth- and eighteenth-century interiors. The scenes depicted were invariably chosen partly for decorative reasons, but rarely for decorative reasons alone.

The key thing to remember when looking up at the loose-limbed characters and creatures of the ancient world is that they would have been familiar to any well-educated Englishman or woman from the late sixteenth to the mid-twentieth century, as a formal education was steeped in the Classical tradition. Classical knowledge at the time was based on a variety of literary sources, one of the most fertile being the world created in the long poem *Metamorphoses* by the Latin poet Ovid. Written *c*.20–10 BC, *Metamorphoses* is a vast collection of mythological stories, each of which involves an element of change or transformation. Anyone really interested in the subject of Classical symbols would find it worthwhile reading *Metamorphoses* in a good translation.

Ovid's stories were adapted by painters and poets as well as playwrights, not least by Shakespeare in his *Midsummer's Night Dream*. *Metamorphoses* similarly supplied popular plots for the opera and court masques; and monarchs were sometimes flattered in poems and paintings by association with the Classical deities or heroes. Queen Elizabeth I, for instance, was identified in poems and paintings as the just Virgin Astraea, described in Book I of Ovid's *Metamorphoses*; while the later ruler, William III, was associated with the mighty hero, Hercules.

The most popular Classical myths were also frequently circulated in pictorial form via contemporary prints and engravings, which provided helpful models for patrons and craftsmen, although no single canonical source seemed to exist.

Among the scenes most commonly seen in country house interiors, love seems to be the enduring one, personified by Venus, the shapely goddess of love, along with her cherubic son Cupid who, poised with love bow and arrows, personified the triumph of love.

Historical figures, such as the Roman emperors, also make numerous appearances in country house interiors, celebrating the martial success of returning British heroes, as seen around the door of seventeenth-century Lulworth Castle in Dorset. In similar vein, the busts of twelve Roman emperors appeared along the façades of Honington Hall and Farnborough Hall in Warwickshire in the mid-eighteenth century. Busts of the emperors were also a popular decorative theme in halls and gardens.

LEFT: A line of Roman emperors, set in niches, embellishes the elevation at Honington Hall in Warwickshire, a late 17th-century house remodelled by Joseph Townsend in the 1740s and 1760s. Renowned Roman rulers remained a popular decorative theme in country houses throughout the 18th century.

References to the glory of arms also appeared, in the form of trophies, or bundles or arms, as can be seen in the hall at Moor Park in Hertfordshire and in the ante-room at Syon Park in Middlesex. Typically, such arms were based on Roman trophies, as displayed on Roman triumphs and illustrated in Roman carving.

IN THE LAND OF THE GODS

CLASSICAL CONCEPTS AND images, inspired by the Italian Renaissance, reached England during the later sixteenth century. An early Elizabethan example of Renaissance inspiration is the carved relief of the Roman sun god Apollo with the Nine Muses, personifying the creative arts, which now appears on the chimneypiece of the withdrawing chamber at Hardwick Hall, having originated at Elizabethan Chatsworth. The theme clearly highlights the love of poetry and music in the Elizabethan country house.

Another Elizabethan example survives in the State Bedchamber of around 1600 at Haddon Hall in Derbyshire where an overmantel shows Orpheus, whose story is described in Book 10 of the *Metamorphoses*. A mortal musician, Orpheus was so skilled that he could charm the animals, birds and trees.

The early seventeenth-century plaster ceiling at Blickling Hall in Norfolk displays a wealth of emblems (images intended to convey a story) drawn from Henry Peacham's *Minerva Britannia* (1612). One shows the goddess Athena being born from the head of Zeus; elsewhere the Greek hero Hercules appears among other gods and mortals.

Some of the later seventeenth-century painted scenes present quite elaborate intellectual schemes. At Chatsworth, for instance, the ceiling of the State Dining Room depicts a battle between Ratio (reason) and Libido (passion), the former represented by Diana, Apollo and Mercury, the latter by Venus and Cupid. It is worth noting, of course, that much of such Classical iconography of the period was casual and light-hearted in spirit.

As well as informing a gentleman's education, the study of Classical culture became a key motive for going on the Grand Tour from the early years of the eighteenth century. Regarded as

RIGHT: *At Burton Constable, Yorkshire, a fine 1760s plaster relief by William Collier depicts Bacchus, god of wine, riding off on a tiger with the beautiful mortal Ariadne.*

FAR RIGHT: *Clearly visible from the bed alcove, the romantic decoration on the ceiling of the King's Bedroom at Compton Place, Sussex, shows Venus and Adonis in amorous embrace, inspired by an episode from Ovid's* Metamorphoses, *Book X.*

a distinct period of education for young noblemen and gentlemen of fortune, the Grand Tour consisted of travels around the great sites of Italy, particularly Rome, in the company of an erudite tutor. The Tour was a regular feature until the end of the century when the Napoleonic wars made travel unsafe. Many Northern European nationals also toured around Italy, but the British formed the most numerous.

On the Grand Tour, young aristocrats were expected to pick up more than a passing interest in the arts and architecture of antiquity. The young 8th Duke of Hamilton wrote: 'I have not read the Roman Classics with so very little feeling as not to wish to view the country which they describe, and where they were written.' Many, however, regarded the tour as only fun in the sun, Lady Mary Wortley Montagu observing that in her view 'the boys only remember where they met with the best wines or the prettiest women'.

The heyday of the tour was enjoyed in a period of peace and prosperity, after the upheavals of the English Civil War, the Restoration and the Glorious Revolution, which brought William III to the throne. It was a boom time for British commerce and unprecedented territorial expansion; indeed, the Georgian upper classes proclaimed themselves the natural heirs of Classical civilization.

On their European travels many young aristocrats acquired paintings, sculptures and antique fragments that still inform the appearance of country houses today. Classical busts were particularly popular, sometimes bought in plaster casts for the halls and libraries at home. It was also customary to have one's portrait painted in front of some suitably fetching Roman ruin, such as the Colosseum, often by an Italian artist, such as Pompeo Batoni. The young men returned home with a better understanding of the sites and sources of the Classical world, which in turn doubtless enhanced their enjoyment of the various naked goddesses decorating the saloon or bedroom, the busts of the ancient poets in the library, and the temples to the Classical gods in the landscape parks outside.

Of the Classical gods, the one most often seen in English country house decor seems to be Bacchus, god of wine, usually depicted as a naked youth crowned in vine leaves and grapes, and

clasping a goblet of wine. Copies in plaster or bronze of Renaissance versions of the god by Jacopo Sansovino or Michelangelo also abound in English collections.

Bacchus is sometimes depicted with Ceres, goddess of the harvest, particularly in the decoration of rooms used for dining, such as the late seventeenth-century saloon at Sudbury Hall in Derbyshire. In the 1760s dining room of Burton Constable in Yorkshire, a full-size figure of Bacchus stood at one end of the room while the plaster panel over the chimneypiece shows Bacchus with the beautiful mortal Ariadne on the back of a tiger. Below the relief runs a swag of Bacchic vine leaves.

Other attributes of Bacchus that might decorate dining rooms include bunches of grapes, ivy leaves, the god's fertility wand tipped with a pinecone, or dancing satyrs (part-goat spirits of the woods). Any one such attribute would have been immediately recognizable to the dinner guests as an allusion to Bacchus. The god himself often sits in as a personification of autumn; with

Ceres, the goddess of corn, as summer; Flora, the goddess of flowers, as spring; and winter personified by an old man wrapped up in a thick cloak and standing by a brazier.

The Latin poet Terence famously observed that without wine and feasting love grows cold: 'Sine Bacchus and Ceres Venus friget', and Bacchus happily disporting himself in the eating rooms of country houses might in some ways be a prelude to love.

Another popular deity, Apollo, the sun god and leader of the Nine Muses, or Arts, often appears with his face framed in a sunburst, sometimes on a chimneypiece in a principal room, such as a saloon or drawing room.

The most commonly represented goddess is Venus, the Roman goddess of love and fertility. The appearance of the beautiful naked figure of Venus on a bedroom ceiling, such as that at Langley Park in Norfolk, surely does not need much explaining. In Classical mythology, Venus is the

LEFT: *The library ceiling relief at Langley Park, Norfolk, depicts the tragic myth of the handsome hunter Actaeon, who unwittingly glimpsed the goddess Diana bathing naked in the forest. For his temerity, he was turned into a stag, hunted down and devoured by his own hounds.*

mother of Cupid, and her attendants are the Three Graces. Among the goddess's many symbols are the shell and dolphin, associated with her legendary birth from the sea; and the doves or swans that drew her chariots. In the absence of the goddess herself, the Three Graces allude to her qualities.

FOR THE LOVE OF VENUS

LOVE STORIES associated with Venus, and related in Ovid's *Metamorphoses*, are depicted in English country house interiors of the late seventeenth and eighteenth centuries. One story, depicted at Easton Neston in Northamptonshire, relates how Venus fell in love with the handsome youth Adonis, after a chance graze from Cupid's arrow. In popular depictions of the myth, Venus is usually shown imploring Adonis to stay with her rather than go off hunting. With embraces and kisses she pleads with him in vain. Adonis strides off to the forest, where he is slain by a wild boar. In her grief, Venus makes his blood spring up as the blood-red anemone. Another story appearing in country houses recounts Venus's seduction of Mars, for example, in the late seventeenth-century painted ceiling in a bedroom at Boughton in Northamptonshire. This scenario signifies the triumph of love over war, perhaps showing that love is greater than war.

Diana, the chaste goddess of hunting (and of marriage), was another popular subject. Hunting has always been one of the favourite pastimes of aristocrats and country gentleman, from the medieval period until our own times. A depiction of a sacrifice being made to Diana (drawn from an engraving of a Classical relief) appears in an overmantel at Ditchley Park in Oxfordshire, also at Clandon Park in Surrey and at Houghton Hall in Norfolk. At Houghton, the home of the politician Sir Robert Walpole, its appearance probably also carried contemporary political significance.

Another myth about the goddess, the tragic story of Diana and Actaeon, is depicted at Langley Park in Norfolk. In the myth described in Ovid's *Metamorphoses*, the young Greek prince Actaeon stumbles on Diana and her nymphs bathing in the nude. As punishment for his unwitting temerity, the fierce goddess turns him into a stag, to be chased and slain by his own hounds.

In another allusion to Diana, which appears on the hall overmantel at Hagley Park in Worcestershire, Pan, god of the fields, flocks and herds, is shown wooing the huntress with a fleece.

RIGHT: *Apollo with his lyre stands welcome in the stone hall at Osterley Park, Middlesex, ushering guests into his world of music and poetry, where the delights of both Bacchus and Venus (the deities of wine and love) would also be enjoyed. The house was designed in the 1760s by Robert Adam for the banker Robert Child.*

A wonderful example of the Georgian obsession with the celebration of love through Classical allusion appears at Danson House, near Bexleyheath in Kent. A fine, recently restored decoration painted by Charles Pavillon in the 1760s celebrates the love of Pomona and Vertumnus, minor deities associated with orchards and farming. In the story related in Book XIV of Ovid's *Metamorphoses*, Vertumnus woos the object of his affections in many rustic disguises, the last being that of an old crone. When Vertumnus at last reveals himself from behind his hideous crone mask Pomona falls for him. At Danson House the story clearly alluded to the love of London merchant John Boyd, an older man, for his young second wife, whose profile appears in a Classical medallion over Danson's front door.

Another occasional source for decoration were the stories from Aesop's *Fables*, sharp moral tales such as that of the Fox and the Crow. Designs for the *Fables* were often based on prints made by Francis Barlow. Some fine examples of the morals appear in various mid-eighteenth-century interiors, such as the library at Kirtlington Park in Oxfordshire, the octagonal saloon at Honington Hall in Warwickshire and the pink parlour at Claydon in Buckinghamshire.

From the 1760s Robert Adam's novel approach to Classical interior decoration was more closely based on authentic Roman examples unearthed by mid-eighteenth-century excavations. Adam's designs, which are rich in depictions of Classical mythology, focus particularly on the gods and goddesses, and on the pagan sacrifices made to them. On the ceilings at Syon Park, for instance, the female dancers and music-makers revolving around the small painted roundels represent festive deities or women performing sacred rituals. Adam's designs can also be admired in the Marble Hall at Kedleston, one of the greatest evocations of Roman architecture in England.

At Osterley Park, designed by Adam, almost every detail of the interior decoration seems to refer to Apollo, Venus and Bacchus (the imagery apparently devised by an Eton schoolmaster for the patron, the banker Robert Child). Even the state bed was designed to be seen as a temple to Venus. The Classical allusions seem to evoke a private Arcadia full of love and happiness, for the delight of the patron, his family and friends.

145

RIGHT: *The magnificent gilded plasterwork ceiling of
the great drawing room at Syon Park, Middlesex, designed
by Robert Adam in 1761, contains countless painted
roundels depicting the Classical myths. At centre top,
for instance, Europa is carried off by Jupiter in the shape
of a great white bull.*

The idea of a Classical Arcadia ruled over by Pan, often alluded to in love poetry, was by no means reserved for the interior. The Arcadian theme also informs the landscape park outside, with its temples dedicated to Venus, Apollo and Flora. Indeed it could be said that the great proliferation of porticoes had turned the country house itself into a kind of temple. By the addition of a portico and colonnade at West Wycombe Park in Buckinghamshire, for example, it was clearly intended to make the house look like a temple in an Arcadian landscape. West Wycombe's mid-eighteenth-century park is so charged with Classical allusions to Venus that it makes one blush to read up the small detail. Suffice it to say that the lake is designed in the shape of a swan, one of Venus's attributes.

Both the great landscape gardens at Stowe in Buckinghamshire and Stourhead in Wiltshire (now with the National Trust) exemplify the way in which the Classical gods were used in the service of pleasure and the curious mixture of seriousness and silliness that they represented. At Stourhead, for instance, a walk around a lake leads to a series of buildings: first a temple dedicated to Flora; then a grotto sheltering a river god and water nymph, sleeping amid the sounds of gushing water; further on a Pantheon appears, guarded by Hercules; and finally there is a temple to Apollo.

At Stowe, Sir Richard Temple, later 1st Viscount Cobham, laid out numerous temples and statues, and as one anonymous author noted in 1738: 'There is scarce a walk in this terrestrial paradise but is terminated by some obelisque, Temple or Masoleum.'

Stowe's gardens abound with various serious and political allusions, as Temple was politically a Whig, strongly believing in the liberties of a system with a constitutional, rather than an absolute, monarch. However, the whole show at Stowe was really for fun. The same author noted of Stowe's temple to Venus: 'one side of the Temple is furnished with altars suitable to the Deity of the Place, viz couches and pillows'.

Classical allusions remained common in neo-Classical interiors up until the early nineteenth century, until they were displaced by a revival of interest in earlier English styles, the medieval, Elizabethan and Jacobean. Although Bacchic grapes continued to decorate dining-room cornices, other Classical themes lost their central place in English interiors.

CHAPTER FOUR

READING THE ROOMS 1200-1750

Medieval to Stuart

THE AIM OF this chapter and the next is to give a sense of the major changes in layout affecting the principal rooms of the English country house; and to highlight some of the main room types associated with particular periods, ranging from the medieval hall, to the elegant suites of the late seventeenth century, on through changing layouts to country houses today that are progressively more informal. It is a general summary, as fashion, funds and personal choices affect the development of each and every country house in different ways. Some houses are built afresh, others adapted, remodelled within or extended, and rooms given different uses and

LEFT: *The awe-inspiring, early 14th-century great hall at Penshurst, Kent, has retained its original central hearth. Such large, multi-purpose spaces lay at the centre of the ceremonial and social life of the great house, indeed, of the local community. Used for dining, entertainment and administration, great halls also served as manor courts.*

RIGHT: One of the finest examples of timber construction, dating from the early 16th century, Rufford Old Hall in Lancashire was built with arched braces rising from short hammer beams, a method enabling the dramatic spans of space seen here. Note also the rare, moveable screen (at centre), highly carved with heraldic and other decoration.

different names with each successive generation, let alone each century. But one theme does emerge, namely the transition from traditional formality and hierarchy towards the comfort and convenience that we take for granted today.

NORMAN TO TUDOR: GREAT HALL AND CHAMBER

WHO CAN RESIST THE CHARMS of the old English manor house? Its very survival excites a particular kind of pleasure, and the remaining manor houses open to the public today often have a special atmosphere, evoked by carefully chosen period furniture, an occasional piece of armour, and a large log burning slowly in the hearth.

With any visit to a well-preserved manor house of the fourteenth and fifteenth centuries one becomes immediately aware of a number of key elements within its overall layout. At its heart lies the great hall with the private family apartments at one end; and at the other end (historically at least) the kitchen and pantry (where bread was kept), and the buttery (where beer was kept). The division was usually marked by what is traditionally called the screens passage, a thoroughly practical piece of design, which screened off the kitchen end, but allowed access, with a certain ceremony, from the kitchen to the hall.

Most manor houses were naturally accompanied by useful supporting buildings. The seventeenth-century author John Aubrey, writing in reference to Bradfield Manor in Wiltshire, described the essential ingredients of what was an admired archetype even then:

> *…the architecture of an old English gentleman's house was a good high strong wall, a gatehouse, and a great hall and parlour; and within, a little green court where you came in, stood, one side the Barn. They then thought not the noise of the threshold ill music.*

The hall, a feature of English life from before the Norman Conquest in 1066, was a place of many purposes. A large rectangular room open to its roof timbers, it was the centre of life at the manor,

the hub of administration and hospitality. Great halls also represented a hierarchical way of life, with the lord's family eating on a raised dais at one end, an arrangement reflected today in Cambridge and Oxford colleges, where master and fellows dine at high table, while the students sit at long tables below. The customary top table at a wedding feast harks back to the same idea.

Earliest halls were aisled rather like some ancient churches, but from the thirteenth century they were more commonly built under a single span. This led to the development of an elaborate roof structure, known as the hammer beam roof, which combined advanced engineering with ornate visual impact, of which early sixteenth-century Rufford Old Hall in Lancashire illustrates the apogee. These great roofs were an essential part of the theatre of aristocratic life.

From at least the twelfth century the hall was accompanied by a private room for the lord and his family, known usually as the great chamber (due to its size), but sometimes also known as a solar. The great chamber was often connected to the great hall by a staircase. Castle architecture of the twelfth to fourteenth centuries might combine great hall, chamber and chapel within the keep, sometimes ranked one above the other.

LEFT: *The elegant 1520s bay window, or oriel, at Hengrave Hall, Suffolk, filled with fine armorial glass, was designed to flood the upper or lord's end of the great hall with light. The beautifully detailed oriel, with its delightfully carved, fan-vaulted ceiling, is almost large enough to form a room in its own right.*

Like the great hall, the great chamber was a room of many functions, and from the thirteenth century it became the norm for the lord, his family and private guests to dine in the great chamber, with the senior household servants sitting at the dais end of the hall – a change lamented by William Langland in his poem *Piers Plowman* of the late fourteenth century:

> *Elynge is the halle eche day in the wyke,*
> *There the lord ne ladye lyketh not to sytte*
> *Now hath each riche a reule to eten by hym-selve*
> *in a pryve-parlour.*

The hall remained a principal room of reception, general waiting room and circulation space (sometimes used for plays and sometimes for holding courts). It was in some ways symbolic of the largesse and status of the lord and, despite the existence of the great chamber, would still be used for larger celebrations. By the fifteenth century, the typical manor house layout had emerged, with a hall set between two wings, one usually containing a chamber over a private parlour, while the other wing included the kitchen, pantry and buttery, with another set of lodgings above.

From the late fourteenth to the sixteenth century, the dais end of the hall was often marked on the outside by a distinctive oriel window (see page 69), such as at Hengrave Hall in Suffolk. The oriel served as a projecting bay, flooding the dais end of the hall with light, and in many cases created almost an additional room.

By the late sixteenth century, the hall was no longer always open to the roof, but often situated on the ground floor with rooms above on the the first floor. In some houses, such as Broughton Castle in Oxfordshire, existing great halls were divided horizontally to create more private accommodation for the family and honoured guests on the first floor.

The hall persisted as a feature of the country house well into the seventeenth century, although by mid-century it had developed, in effect, into a grand entrance hall, with servants eating in other defined quarters (see pages 188–9) that became known as the servants' hall.

ELIZABETHAN TO JACOBEAN: THE GREAT CHAMBER AND LONG GALLERY

O N CIRCUITING AN Elizabethan or Jacobean manor house, a visitor today notices first on the outside the tall façades and extended symmetrical bays or wings. Immediately inside, the hall of status seems not unlike that in a medieval manor, but on wandering around the house, the visitor becomes aware, too, of additional rooms of distinction on the upper floors, approached by much more open and substantial staircases than in medieval houses.

By the sixteenth century, the great chamber had become the central focus of the manor house, at the heart of the household, where the family entertained friends and important visitors.

OPPOSITE: *The rich decoration in the great chamber at Chastleton in Oxfordshire, built c. 1614, illustrates the room's central importance in the life of the manor. Serving as the principal living room for the lord, his family and honoured guests, the great chamber could also double up as sleeping quarters.*

ABOVE: *One of the finest surviving examples, the long gallery at Haddon Hall, Derbyshire, was built in the middle of the 16th century, and altered c. 1603. A place for parade and promenade, for walking and talking in wet weather, the long gallery was also a forerunner of the 18th- and 19th-century picture gallery.*

RIGHT: *The handsome long gallery at Little Moreton
Hall in Cheshire, a magnificent timber-framed house,
was added to the top of the gatehouse wing in the 1580s.
Enjoying views from both sides, it is also richly decorated
with plaster reliefs at either end, one depicting Destiny,
and the other, the Wheel of Fortune.*

Inevitably, too, it was the most decorated part of the manor, lavished with the most permanent
decoration, such as carved chimneypieces, plasterwork and panelling.

During the sixteenth century it is quite usual to find a dedicated parlour for everyday private
dining, as well as additional small family parlours, which also doubled up as bedchambers,
sometimes arranged in suites. By the early seventeenth century, Gainsborough Old Hall, for
instance, was described in a 1625 inventory as having a 'Little Dining Parlour, Little Side Parlour,
Garden Parlour and Great Parlour'.

The principal innovation of the sixteenth century, persisting well into the seventeenth century,
was the long gallery, which became a key feature of the Elizabethan and Jacobean country house,
from Little Moreton Hall in Cheshire, to Hatfield House in Hertfordshire. In 1531 a Venetian
visitor to Whitehall Palace in London observed that it had 'three so-called galleries, which are
long porticoes or halls with windows on either side looking on rivers and gardens'. One of the
earliest surviving long galleries dating from the 1520s can be seen at The Vyne in Hampshire.

The long gallery was usually, in effect, a top-floor exercise space, with views over gardens and
into the distance, but also a place for private conversation. It is not difficult to imagine many of
the intimate conversations that feature in Shakespeare's plays taking place in a long gallery, like
the one at Haddon Hall in Derbyshire.

Even in the later seventeenth century the architect Sir Roger North still described the long
gallery as 'a room for no other use but pastime and health', which created a space for 'select
companys to converse in'. Like the great hall, the long gallery was an important status symbol
often accorded the richest decoration available, such as the provision at Blickling Hall in Norfolk
of a breathtakingly long plasterwork ceiling that seems to disappear into the distance.

The long gallery also served as an early picture gallery, where most of the pictures were hung.
Perhaps by virtue of its scale the long gallery quickly became the natural repository for portraits,
displaying prestigious family alliances (established or desired) to anyone admitted for
entertainment in the family's grandest rooms. Thomas Howard wrote in 1609 of his own gallery
where he planned to display: 'pictures of sundry of my honourable friends, whose presentation

thereby to behold will greatly delight me to walk often in that place where I may see so comfortable a sight'.

One of the finest Elizabethan long galleries, dating from the 1590s, can be seen at Hardwick Hall in Derbyshire. It is a great stately room of unusual height with ranks of tall windows, richly hung even now with tapestries and family portraits. The long gallery tradition continued into the Jacobean era, with many ornately decorated examples, as at Aston Hall in Warwickshire and Knole in Kent. A late seventeenth-century example, now thought to have been a deliberate evocation of the early seventeenth-century tradition, can be seen at Sudbury Hall in Derbyshire.

STUART TO EARLY GEORGIAN: THE BEST OR GREAT APARTMENT

WHEN VISITING THE great stately country houses of the later seventeenth and early eighteenth centuries, any visitor will immediately become aware of the deliberate formality of the layout of the major reception rooms, characterized by a certain self-conscious stateliness. The new style of formality reflected a radical shift in country house planning involving a new concept – the 'great apartment', a suite of rooms laid out with formal grandeur in a straight line, creating a sense of privileged progression through layers of privacy.

The great apartment usually consisted of an ante-room, withdrawing room, bedroom and closet. At both Petworth in Sussex and Beninbrough in Yorkshire, the main public reception rooms lie at the centre of the house, with the great apartments extending away on either side. The lofty and elegant rooms of the great apartment run in a straight line with their tall doors carefully aligned, often on the window sides, creating a magnificent sense of repetition, distance and grandeur. The straight line cutting through richly framed doorcases is known as an *enfilade*, from the French word for threading or piercing along a straight line.

When any visitor called on the occupant of the great apartment, how far he or she progressed through the suite of rooms was an indication of either their own high status or their particular relationship with the occupants of the rooms. The visitor might be made to wait in the antechamber, or invited through to the withdrawing room, to the bedchamber and even into the

LEFT: *The lavish King's Bedchamber at Powis Castle, Powys, illustrates the late 17th-century Baroque apartment system, in which a series of richly decorated rooms was laid out in a line, culminating in the most private and privileged room, the bedroom, with entry to each room achieved by rank. As the bedroom was also used as a sitting room, the bed compartment or bed alcove was often railed, as seen here at Powis.*

cabinet. The bedchamber, as in previous centuries. was a room used for sleeping, eating and entertaining, even private dining. The formal layout of such rooms reflected the great power of aristocratic patronage of the day.

The key influence behind the shift in style was the French court of King Louis XIV, whose great royal chateau at Versailles exemplifies the formal layout. The French model included a large room for grand entertainment, the equivalent of the old hall, known as the *salle* or saloon, set in the centre of a Classically designed house, with a balancing sequence of apartments on either side.

At the grandest end of the scale the great apartment included a state bedroom for a king's visit, the best surviving example of which exists at Powis Castle in Wales, where a bed is set in a recess and railed off with a low carved balustrade. The small private room off the bedchamber was usually called a closet or cabinet, and provided the ultimate privacy. In Whitehall Palace Charles II used his

LEFT: *At Chatsworth, Derbyshire, the most immediately noticeable architectural impact of the Baroque apartment system is the alignment of doors and windows, creating the* enfilade, *a repetitive but elegant effect suggestive of grandeur and ritual that persisted well into the 18th century.*

RIGHT: *The queen's closet at Ham House, Surrey, is one of the finest surviving examples of a late 17th-century closet, with a ceiling decorated by Antonio Verrio. The closet or dressing room provided the most intimate space in state apartments of the period.*

cabinet to talk in private to his trusted ministers, a custom that gave rise to our term 'cabinet government'. One of the finest late seventeenth-century closets can be seen at Ham House in Surrey.

Chatsworth in Derbyshire was remodelled in the French formality for William Cavendish, 4th Earl and 1st Duke of Devonshire (who was instrumental in inviting William III and Mary to take the throne). The duke created a grand 'state' apartment of astonishing richness. As the new state apartment was created within the old long gallery of the originally Elizabethan house, a mirror was placed at the end of the suite to create a reflection that would extend the dramatic visual effect – it remains a dazzling sight today.

Many variations on the basic formula arose, reflecting the same sense of progression and privileged privacy described. The concept was reinforced by an increasing richness of decoration culminating in the awe-inspiring state beds of the age (see the glorious example from Melville House, now in the British Galleries of the Victoria and Albert Museum, or the fine green velvet state bed at Houghton Hall in Norfolk).

Although from the 1720s English country house design fell under the influence of Italian Palladian architecture (see page 51), the basic layout still reflected in varied forms the late seventeenth-century formal arrangement of grand apartments on the first floor (known as the *piano nobile*), on either side of a hall and saloon. The ground floor, often called the rustic storey, usually contained the less formal everyday withdrawing rooms and a dining room for family use, as well as the kitchen and servants' rooms (see page 186).

Describing one of the grand bi-annual congresses held at Houghton by Sir Robert Walpole, John Lord Hervey observed in July 1731:

> *…the base or the rustick story, is what is chiefly inhabited at the Congress. There is a room for breakfast, another for supper, another for dinner, another for afternooning, and the great arcade with four-chimneys for walking and quid-nuncing [Latin for 'What now?' referring to the fine old art of gossiping] … while above he said lay: 'the floor of taste, expense, state and parade'…*

LEFT: *Lavishly decorated in Louis XV style, the Elizabeth Saloon at Belvoir Castle, Rutland, reflects the revival of French fashion at the end of the Napoleonic War. One of a sequence of grand rooms created in the 19th century, it stands in deliberate contrast to adjoining Chinese and Gothic-style interiors.*

CHAPTER FIVE

READING THE ROOMS 1750-1910

Georgian to Edwardian

GEORGIAN ROOMS: CIRCUITS OF PURE PLEASURE

Visitors to Georgian country houses of the mid- to late eighteenth century are often struck by their elegant proportions and dignified interiors, regarded by many as a high point in English architecture. But any visitor already familiar with the earlier lofty elegance of the 'great apartment' (see page 158) will sense a subtle shift in atmosphere and layout. Instead of the formal symmetry of the great apartment, planned on *enfilade*, the rooms of the later Georgian era were laid out on a new type of 'circuit plan'. The shift between the formal symmetry of the earlier apartment plan and the relaxed layout of the later circuit plan was a gradual one.

In the new circuit plan, the key rooms for entertaining were designed in a circuit (often around a top-lit staircase), a form that seems to have been established initially in great London houses, such as Norfolk House. The rooms were designed to be capable of hosting substantial numbers of people at one event, as entertaining in the country grew in popularity, partly because of the changing nature of political patronage and partly as a result of improved transport.

RIGHT: *Serving as both ballroom and picture gallery,
the grand saloon at Saltram, Devon, was designed in
1768 by Robert Adam for the type of lavish entertaining
that developed in the later 18th century. Saltram's stylish
saloon exemplifies the coordinated detailing of carpet and
ceiling characteristic of Adam interiors.*

The second generation of Palladian architects, led by Sir Robert Taylor and Sir William Chambers, had developed the Classical Roman ideal of the villa (see page 32). Its raised ground floor/first floor, based on the Italian model, now often contained a drawing room, library and dining room grouped around a central top-lit staircase hall.

Instead of being strung out in a long line, the principal rooms presented a progress, and indeed sometimes filled most of an elevation each, with the added advantage of canted (three-sided) bays and bow windows that enjoyed a fine aspect onto the surrounding landscape. Sir Robert Taylor's houses, including Harleyford Manor in Buckinghamshire, Barlaston Hall in Staffordshire and the recently restored Danson House in Kent, illustrate this type clearly.

With the circuit plan, the sequence of rooms on the main floor could be used for comfortable everyday living, but could also be easily converted to rooms of entertainment whenever a party was held. A drawing room, library and dining room could be transformed into card room, ballroom and supper room for social events. From this time on, the library became an important informal drawing room. Indeed, a house plan had emerged that seems eminently livable to modern eyes.

Houses on a larger scale include Kedleston and Robert Adam's adaptations of great houses, such as Osterley and Syon, with their impressive series of great rooms devised for entertaining large numbers in a well-planned and elegant circuit. Inspired by his travels to Rome, Adam added visual drama to the basic circuit plan by designing rooms in varied shapes, some round and some rectangular or bow-ended, in some ways reflecting the varied effects created by the different rooms within a Roman Bath complex. Adam also designed the handsome sculpture gallery at Newby Hall in Yorkshire, which serves as a good example of the late eighteenth-century fashion for displaying sculptures acquired on the Grand Tour.

The creation of visual contrasts was further developed by Sir John Soane, who used shallow domes and top lighting (to create what he referred to as 'the poetry of architecture') in hundreds of alterations to country houses, such as the Yellow Drawing Room at Wimpole Hall in Cambridgeshire, and Moggerhanger in Bedfordshire.

An insight into the nature of the society that the country house represented at this date emerges in Robert Adam's introduction to his *Works in Architecture* (1773), where he compared the English and French dining habits:

> *Accustomed by habit, or indeed induced by the nature of our climate, we
> indulge more largely in the enjoyment of the bottle. Every person of rank here
> is either a member of the legislation, or entitled by his rank to take part in the
> political arrangements of his country, and to enter with ardour into those
> discussions to which they give rise.*

Political debate, Adam argued, gave a new importance to the status of the dining room and, in turn, to the drawing room, for 'these circumstances lead men to live more with one another, and more detached from the society of ladies', who withdrew to the drawing room. The key roles of dining and drawing rooms would develop more fully during the Regency era until well into the early twentieth century.

Another key transition in the early nineteenth century was the gradual disappearance of the highly visible 'rustic' or raised basement floor, which had always meant that the main reception rooms were on a raised ground floor or first floor. From the later eighteenth century the main reception rooms were situated on the ground floor and the basement level sunk down beneath. This new layout is illustrated by the work of Henry Holland at Berrington Hall in Herefordshire, where the service wing is sited discreetly to one side, but is still part of the overall design.

Sir William Chambers' Duddingstone outside Edinburgh, designed in 1762, was one of the first notable Palladian-inspired country houses to omit the basement storey and have the columns rise from the ground level. It was an important moment for the country house, when it stepped down off its basement and joined the level of the garden. This connection with the outside, the pleasures of park and garden, was actively pursued by early nineteenth-century designers.

By 1824, indeed, the idea of the earlier raised basement floor had come to seem unattractive to contemporary architects, such as C. R. Cockerell, who described the conventional Palladian country house in unappealing terms:

> *This is a house built for a city – all the architecture be raised, the lower part looking like a prison, the windows inaccessible, uninviting & no communication whatever with the garden or lawn. There is none of that confidence, that palatial and garden look so delightful to encounter with the residence of a country gent.*

REGENCY COMFORT ZONES

THE REGENCY country house (of the early years of the nineteenth century) illustrates the development of the country house as a temple to domestic comforts and civilized entertainment. This is the era of the assemblies and entertainments evoked so memorably in the novels of Jane Austen, and of the growth of the extended house party and the comfortable furnishing of bedrooms.

One American traveller, Louis Simond, wrote of a visit to the Lake District in 1810:

> *…there are no retired places in England, no place where you can see only the country and countrymen: you meet in the country everywhere town-people elegantly dressed and lodged, having a number of servants, and exchanging invitations. England in short seems to be the country house of London; cultivated for amusement only, and where all is subservient to picturesque luxury and ostentation.*

BELOW: *The comfortable dining room at Scampston
Hall, Yorkshire, illustrates the important role that dining
occupied in the late 18th-century/Regency period. The
provision of a handsome sideboard in a recess framed by
columns (LEFT) is a typical Regency detail.*

LEFT: *In the magnificent, imaginatively restored dining room at Goodwood House, Sussex, guests could enjoy the glamour of fine dining within an atmosphere of exotic Egyptian antiquity, a taste stimulated by Napoleon's Nile campaign in the 1800s. Originally a Jacobean house, Goodwood was remodelled by James Wyatt for the 3rd Duke of Richmond during the Regency era.*

The Prince Regent himself, who improved the quality of bedrooms at Windsor Castle and enjoyed staying at his friends' houses, encouraged the fashion for country house parties. While many Regency country houses seem breathtakingly grand there was a degree of informality in entertainment, reflected in the sketches made by J. M. W. Turner while staying at Petworth House in Sussex, but also in many diary accounts.

In his *English Tour* (1827) Prince Pückler-Muskau described an evening at Cobham Hall in Kent:

> ...our suffering host lay on the sofa, dozing a little; five ladies and gentlemen were very attentively reading in various sorts of books (of this number I was one, having some views of parks before me): another had been playing for a quarter of an hour with a long suffering dog: two old Members of Parliament were disputing vehemently about the 'Corn Bill' – and the rest of the company were in a dimly lighted room adjoining where a pretty girl was playing on the piano-forte and another with a most perforating voice, singing ballads.

The drawing room and the dining room became firmly established as the two main entertaining rooms. The drawing room was a place to assemble before dinner and for the ladies to withdraw to after dinner, often separated from the dining room by the hall, to keep the raucous noises of gentlemanly drinking at a distance. The Regency dining room was often a spacious and elegant room capable of seating 30 or 40 guests.

The hour of dining had become progressively later and dining rooms were often decorated in darker colours that worked well by candlelight, of which an excellent example survives in the Egyptian-style dining room at Goodwood House in Sussex, recently imaginatively restored. The grand solid mahogany sideboard, a product of the Regency love of dining, was a development of the side-table introduced into the dining rooms of Robert Adam and James Wyatt (see page 214).

RIGHT: The typical High Victorian dining room at Tyntesfield, Somerset, enjoys 'Tudorbethan'-style fittings and furnishings adapted to the needs of 19th-century country house life. In Victorian country houses, dining rooms were unmistakably masculine affairs, with the drawing room usually cast in more feminine character.

While the dining room conceivably took on a more masculine character during the Regency era, the drawing room by contrast became a more feminine zone, reflected in both furniture and decoration.

The library continued to be the most important informal family sitting room and to be furnished with sofas and writing tables, as one contemporary visitor noted of the 1819 library at Althorp: 'sofas, chairs, tables of every comfortable and commodious form are of course liberally scattered throughout the room'. Another good example of a Regency library can be found at Tatton Park in Cheshire. At Sheringham in Norfolk, dating from 1812–19, the architect Humphry Repton designed a smaller country house for a young couple with one large library-cum-living room as well as 'the gentleman's own room, for games, papers and Justice business' but 'no useless drawing room'.

Entrances were almost always found on the same level as the park. Humphry Repton pioneered easier links between the house, garden and landscape, supplying many designs for conservatories and French windows. The conservatory thus became another key room in the Regency era, when it was not just a room to keep plants, but became an extension of the living spaces of the houses. Some conservatories were arranged as extended winter corridors, where family and guests could walk together in bad weather, as at Sezincote in Gloucestershire, designed by S. P. Cockerell and Thomas Daniell. Incidentally it was Repton's introduction of John Nash to the Prince Regent to design a conservatory at Brighton that led to Nash's work on the Brighton Pavilion, Regent's Park and Buckingham Palace.

VICTORIAN AND EDWARDIAN: THE AGE OF LUXURY

VICTORIAN COUNTRY HOUSES are among the glories of England. Built in their thousands when the British Empire was expanding, and British commerce, industry and agriculture were all moving on an upward graph, the Victorian country house, for the most part, seems well built and planned, but came in a surprising variety of shapes, sizes and styles. A particular development in Victorian times was the use of specialized functional space, dictated by advances

PREVIOUS PAGES: *The grand parlour of Wightwick Manor, Staffordshire, designed by Edward Ould in the 1890s, illustrates the late Victorian revival of the great hall as a popular living room at the heart of the house, complete with bay window heavy with armorial stained glass.*

ABOVE: *The classic billiard room, exemplified at Eastnor Castle, Herefordshire, was a* sine qua non *of the 19th-century country house. The Victorian architect Stevenson observed: 'A billiard room is an essential of most country houses, as a means of killing time on wet days. Its position should be retired so that men may be at their ease in it smoking and playing in their shirt sleeves'.*

in plumbing that might, for instance, fix the use of some rooms, such as the bathroom, in contrast to the more flexible way in which rooms were clearly used in previous centuries.

In many ways the Victorian country house plan was an elaboration of the Regency type developed in the early nineteenth century, with the drawing room, dining room and library serving as key reception rooms. The Victorian model differs in catering for an increased expectation of comfort, and in the number of dedicated rooms, created for specific social purposes, such as smoking.

The new dedicated rooms divide into four main areas: firstly the revival of the great hall; secondly special rooms for male hospitality (billiards room, smoking room and gun room); thirdly the nursery floor; and fourthly the increasingly specialized servants' and service quarters. These additions, the servants' wing in particular, also played their part in creating the spreading, asymmetrical plan that we tend to associate with the Victorian country house.

The revival of the great hall had also begun in the early nineteenth century. It was in great part symbolic of the period's industrial revolution and new wealth. There was something handsome and reassuring about a room that recalled the glorious English past when the lord of the manor, his family and household had dined under one roof. When designing the hall at Scarisbrick Hall for the Earl of Shrewsbury, the great Victorian Gothic Revival architect A. W. N. Pugin observed: 'As regards the hall I have nailed my colours to the mast – a bay window, high open roof, two good fireplaces, a great sideboard, screen, minstrel gallery – all or none. I will not sell myself to do a wretched thing.'

In 1841, Pugin revealed his essentially nostalgic ideal of the hall when he wrote that 'under the rafters of their capacious halls the lord[s] of the manor used to assemble all their friends and tenants'. In the mid-nineteenth century the great hall was as likely to be a grand entrance hall as anything, but it was, of course, a useful entertaining space for large events, coming-of-age parties and annual tenants' dinners (as at Lismore Castle in Ireland designed by Pugin for the 6th Duke of Devonshire). But in the later nineteenth century such large halls were often developed as a general informal sitting room suitable for after-dinner entertainments for larger house parties.

RIGHT: *Recently restored, the sumptuous, late 19th-century
state bedroom at Waddesdon Manor, Buckinghamshire,
with its dazzling bed and carved 'boiserie' panelling,
exemplifies the richness of 'le goût Rothschild'.*

By 1904 the German architectural critic Herman Muthesius could write how the hall was the
'centre of great memories of a proud past … It represents one of the most attractive assets of the
English house. One steps out of wild nature straight into a warm, friendly atmosphere.' In some
houses the hall 'assumed the character of a real living room … often with a grand piano and a
billiard table'. It was usually, Muthesius thought, 'the favourite room of all'.

Historians have referred to the Victorian country house as 'the moral house' because of the
concern for the segregation of the sexes, particularly at house parties. The 'bachelors' wing', for
instance, was designed for unmarried guests, of which one of the best-appointed examples can
be found at Waddesdon Manor in Buckinghamshire. Bachelors' rooms would be convenient
for (even connected to) very distinctively Victorian billiard and smoking rooms, sometimes
combined as one.

Both billiard and smoking room would inevitably be designed with a rather masculine air,
with the wood panelling and comfortable leather armchairs commonly associated today with the
clubroom. In a billiard room there would usually be leather seats or benches, sometimes on a
raised plinth to allow a better view of the game, and hung paintings of race horses or hunting
scenes. In the last decades of the century, the fashion for shooting parties meant that a gun room
would often complete the male set of rooms.

The drawing room became even more emphatically the territory of ladies in the nineteenth
century, and also became distinctly more formal, reserved for receiving visitors and the social
ceremonies of afternoon tea and for withdrawing after dinner. Smaller sitting rooms evolved for
family use, including a morning room.

The other naturally more feminine territory was the nursery floor where the children would
sleep, play and be educated until sent away to school, the boys usually at an earlier age than the
girls. Quarters for the governess or the nurse might also exist depending on the children's age.
The nursery was sometimes found on a floor of a wing devoted to the family's private use,
separated from the guest rooms, which sometimes occupied a separate wing on the other side of
the communal reception rooms.

LEFT: *The great Victorian kitchen at Lanhydrock, Cornwall, was designed in the 1880s by Richard Coad, with a high ceiling reminiscent of a great hall. Such kitchens lay at the centre of a great complex of rooms devoted to cleaning and food preparation.*

CHAPTER SIX

SERVICING THE COUNTRY HOUSE

Servants

FOR CENTURIES country houses depended on servants for much that in modern life is supplied by technology, such as heat, light, water, cleaning, communication and all sorts of comfort and convenience. Thus, alongside the expansion of grand, decorated interiors with their display of craftsmanship and luxury, rooms were developed for the people who made all that comfort and dignity possible: the servants.

The nature of service and the role of servants changes dramatically over the centuries, reflecting the changing relationships in society and shifting attitudes to the functions and functioning of a great house, its hospitality and privacy. Great medieval households were run by large numbers of servants, sometimes hundreds, whose very number was a visible expression of status; the higher servants would be drawn from the ranks of the local nobility and gentry. Most young noblemen would be attached to a local great house for a period of service as an 'officer of the household', which formed part of their education. By the early eighteenth century, the gentle-born household officer had disappeared and most servants were women.

RIGHT: Original footmen's uniforms being worn in the grand saloon at Osterley Park, Middlesex. Bright livery made footmen the most visible of large households of servants. Livery was derived from among the colours of a family's coat of arms.

Servants still played a ceremonial role in the display of status, however, particularly the footmen dressed in fine livery. Attendant footmen – often over 6ft (1.85m) tall – were chosen for how good they looked in livery. A footman's duties included attending his employer on his travels and carrying messages, as well as some additional attendance in the house.

The novelist Daniel Defoe felt that women should also be in uniform:

> *I remember I was put very much to the Blush, being at a Friends house and by him required to salute the ladies, and I kiss'd the Chamber Jade into the bargain, for she was as well dressed as the best. Things of this Nature would be easily avoided, if servant maids were to wear Liveries.*

In 1777 the Prime Minister Lord North levied a tax on male servants, 1 guinea a head, plus in 1786 a tax on hair powder, which made the wearing of livery more expensive, suggesting that a footman was regarded as an expensive luxury.

A remarkable picture of servant life in a Welsh country house emerged at Erdigg in the 1790s, where a series of portraits commissioned by the squire Phillip Yorke portrays the servants of the house, with acompanying verse, celebrating their contribution to the squire and his family's well being. Successive servants from the late nineteenth and early twentieth centuries were also commemorated in 1911 by a set of photographic portraits and verses hung in the servants' hall.

One of Erdigg's late eighteenth-century portraits depicts the 'kitchen watcher' Jack Nicholas, who is described in rhyming verse as:

> *him that waited on the cook,*
> *and many a walk to Wrexham took,*
> *Whether the Season cold or hot,*
> *A constant porter to the pot:*
>
> *Then in the kitchen corner stuck,*
> *he plucked the fowl and drew the duck,*
> *or with the basket on his knees*
> *was sheller-general to the peas.*

BELOW: *In the servants' hall at Erdigg, Wales (photographed here in 1973 before the National Trust's restoration), the 18th-century portraits and accompanying verse biographies offer an unparalleled insight into the lives of household servants and estate staff.*

The highly organized staffing of country houses reached something of a peak in the later nineteenth century, with each servant performing specifically ordained duties. Indoor staff numbered up to 50 in the bigger ducal houses. In the middle of the century, it is believed, one in three girls between the ages of 15 and 20 was in domestic service.

By 1880 *The Servant's Practical Guide* calculated that, 'The largest establishments – those of noblemen and commoners of great wealth – usually comprise upwards of thirty servants, irrespective of gamekeepers and gardeners.' The make-up of the servants of such a household included 'men-servants … house steward, a groom of the chambers, a butler, a valet, a man cook, three footmen, a head coachman, second coachman, two or three grooms, according to the number of horses'.

The women servants of such a household would number:

> …*a housekeeper, a head lady's maid, an under lady's maid …a head nurse,*
> *a cook (if a man cook is not kept) a head house-maid, two or three under house-*
> *maids, a head laundry-maid, two under-laundry maids, a head kitchen-maid,*
> *a scullery-maid, a vegetable-maid, one or two still room maids, an under nurse,*
> *a nursery maid and a schoolroom maid.*

Households with an income of £40,000 a year and over would employ 30 servants or more, whereas lesser squires probably ran households of around 10 servants.

But while some households enjoyed such large teams of servants well into the early twentieth century, by the time the *Servant's Practical Guide* was published in 1880, the tide had already turned. Agricultural depression, taxation, and the attraction of other careers, which did not proscribe personal freedom in the same degree as that of a late nineteenth-century household servant, contributed to the fall in the number of servants. The final economic and social upheavals of the mid-twentieth century, combined with not a few useful labour-saving devices, meant that even in the grandest houses, only a small team would be employed, as today. Few would live-in, and when they did would expect to be provided with cottages or proper flats rather than simply rooms.

Just think how quiet these country houses must have seemed in the 1950s and 1960s to the generation that had grown up in the 1890s and early 1900s. Moreover, while in National Trust houses and in many great country houses the kitchens are open to the public, in many smaller country houses the useful servants' wing has become a private wing into which the family can retire, leaving the principal rooms open to the public.

Servants' Quarters

In MEDIEVAL MANORS and castles, most servants slept in dormitories, on pallets (straw beds from the French *paille* for straw). Such dormitories were sometimes called barracks, as at Broughton Castle in Oxfordshire, and were very much like the shared bedrooms of soldiers. Barracks remained a feature of country house life well into the nineteenth century, and shared rooms were still the norm until the early twentieth century. William Harrison described the straw pallets in his *Description of England* in the 1570s: '…if they had any sheet above them it was well for seldom had they under their bodies to keep them from the pricking straws that ran oft through the canvas of the pallet and raised their hardened hides'.

In the medieval period some servants clearly slept in rooms close to their master or mistress, perhaps as much for security as for convenience. Sir Henry Wootton in his biography of Lord Buckingham refers to how 'his secretary was laid in a pallet near him for the ventilation of his thoughts'. The curtaining of the traditional four-poster bed may well be partly explained for reasons of privacy. A servant's bed could be stored underneath during the day.

Again in the medieval house, servants usually ate in the great hall, under the eyes of the steward, although in some great houses there appear to have been two halls, one probably for the needs of the household and the other for guests. By the late seventeenth century a dedicated servants' hall had emerged at basement level; this was often effectively a ground floor. Coleshill in Berkshire was one of the first houses with a servants' hall on the ground floor/basement level, along with the kitchen. In 1696, Sir Roger North observed in his writings on architecture:

> It is but late that servants have left their eating in the hall. This in my time was done at my father's house. But since it hath bin usuall, to find a room elsewhere for them; and the master, in summer especially, leaves his little parlor to eat there…

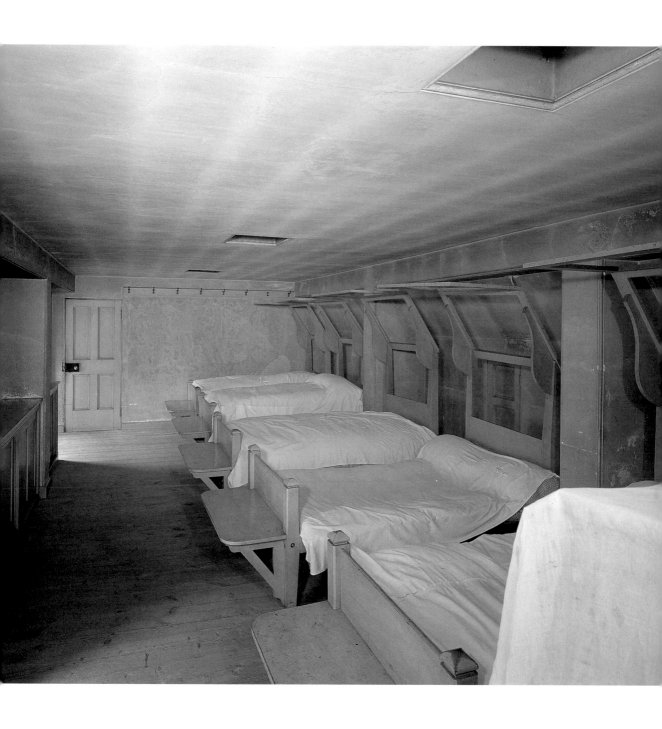

ABOVE: *The servants' barracks at Mamhead House, Devon, designed by Anthony Salvin in the early 1830s. Shared bedrooms remained the norm for servants in large households until well into the early 20th century.*

The creation of a servants' hall was part of the process of separating out the family and the staff, or at least the movement of slops around the house. Instead of the status of a household being shown by visible supporters, servants began to be kept separate. North also observed in 1696:

> *…an inviolable rule to have the entrata in the middle. But this must not be the common passage for all things, in regard your friends and persons of esteem should pass without being annoyed with the sight of foul persons and things, which must and will be moving in some part of a large and well inhabited dwelling. Therefore, for such occasions there must be a back entrata.*

The same rule, North argued, applied to stairs.

The servants' hall and beyond

From the later seventeenth century onwards, servants' sleeping quarters were often sited in the attic storey, sometimes divided up into separate rooms, sometimes into dormitories, perhaps of five or so servants to one room. Sometimes in smaller gentry houses a servants' garret would be barely bigger than the volume of a dormer window. Some household staff would have been accommodated in the stable yard. At Erdigg in the 1720s, for example, servants' quarters comprised two servants' halls on the basement level, as well as 15 beds for maids in the attic room and eight beds for men in the stables and outhouses.

Clearly, grooms and coachmen were regarded as indoor, rather than outdoor, staff, and sometimes doubled up as footmen, as noted by Prince Pückler-Muskau in his *English Tour* (1827):

> *England is the true land of contrasts 'du haut' and 'de bas' at every step. Thus even in elegant houses in the country coachmen and grooms wait at dinner, and are not always free of the odour of the stable.*

But the key room for servants, where they spent most of their daily life, was the servants' hall, usually with the butler's and housekeeper's rooms adjoining. The butler was in charge of the male servants and the housekeeper in charge of the female staff. In 1904 Herman Muthesius noted of the typical servants' hall: 'it is a large, long room; it must be as near the kitchen as possible but at the same time the butler and housekeeper must be able to keep an eye on it from their rooms. It is used not only as a dining room, but also a communal sitting room.'

The servants' hall was also a room in which visiting tradesmen might be received and where the visiting staff of house guests would be entertained. It is interesting to note that servants dining in larger houses often preserved elements of hierarchical tradition, such as the custom for higher servants to take their pudding course in the housekeeper's room rather than with the rest of the servants. Food and board was a key perk of a servant's life, although it is very difficult to credit the story told by Lady Augusta Fane in *Chit Chat* (1926) that one Earl of Derby complained to his butler about the badness of his dinner and said gravely: 'I do not expect to have as good food as you have in the housekeeper's room, but I must insist on it being the same as in the servants' hall.'

Kitchens: Cooking for Quality

CENTRAL TO THE household servant's role was the smooth running of the kitchen and related rooms connected with the preparation, cooking and serving of food, such as the pantry, buttery and bakery. In the earliest manor houses food was possibly cooked over the central hearth, but in most known examples the kitchen seems to have been in a separate building, which was not incorporated into the main house until the fifteenth century. Some very grand thirteenth- and fourteenth-century kitchens were housed in substantial detached buildings, the most advanced of the day being the Abbot's kitchen at Glastonbury or the monastic kitchen at Durham. Both have fine fire-proof stone roofs, representing the most expensive kitchens possible for the period.

RIGHT: *The great Elizabethan kitchen at Burghley House, Lincolnshire, was high-ceilinged, both to accommodate heat and activity but also to express the tradition of largesse and hospitality that was required of a great house.*

Even after the inclusion of the kitchen in the main body of the house, food preparation mostly took place in outbuildings and only the kitchen itself was within the structure of the house. The main kitchen was separated from the great hall by a screens passage, the central opening of which led through to the kitchen. The arrival of food into the great hall included a ceremonial element that is quite difficult for the modern mind to imagine.

The great kitchens were often built on a large scale, and cooking was done first on a huge central hearth and then on a great open fireplace, with smoke escaping through a louvre in the roof. The scale of kitchen and fireplace was devised to mediate the heat and smoke of spit-roasting but also perhaps to reflect the grandeur of the house (see for example the great sixteenth-century kitchens at Hampton Court and Burghley House in Lincolnshire).

The two other arches of the screens passage led to rooms called the pantry and the buttery. In the pantry bread was kept and in the buttery, beer and candles were stored. The kitchen would have been supported by a small courtyard storage room, brewhouse and bakery. The surviving Tudor kitchens at Hampton Court are now brilliantly presented to show how they would have appeared while in use in the sixteenth century.

WHERE SHOULD THE KITCHEN GO?

IN SOME LATE sixteenth- and early seventeenth-century country houses, the kitchen had been arranged on the basement floor, as at Heath Old Hall in Yorkshire, *c.* 1580s, or Chastleton House in Oxfordshire, *c.* early 1600s, where the kitchens usually connected with a central courtyard. It was also the opinion of the influential Italian architectural theorist Palladio that the ground floor semi-basement level of a house should be used for kitchens and pantries.

But Sir Henry Wootton doubted the wisdom of the Italian practice, observing in 1624: 'I have marked a willingnesse, in the Italian Artisans to destribute the Kychin, Pantrie, Bakehouse, washing Roomes: and even Buttrie likewise, under ground.' This he concedes removes some 'annoyes' out of sight and 'adde Majestie to the whole Aspect', but 'by the natural Hospitalitie of

England, the Buttrie must be more visible; and wee neede perchance for our Raunges, a more spacious and luminous Kitchin, then the forsaid Compartition will beare'.

Sir Roger Pratt's note-books on architecture, *c.* 1665, focused on efficient order and organization: 'viz: the kitchen and all its offices to lie together, and the buttery and cellar, with theirs, etc and all these to be disposed of in a half ground storey with their back courts convenient to them'. Elsewhere, he advised:

> *Let your kitchen be placed at the end near your little parlour, yet so that you*
> *above shall not be disturbed with the least noise or smell from thence, but not*
> *so far off that your meat will be cold in bringing from it, or your servant's not*
> *presently at hand upon the least ringing.*

From the early eighteenth century it was not uncommon to find the kitchen arranged not on the basement level any longer but in an adjoining pavilion connected to the main house by a passage.

OPPOSITE: *The scullery at Lanhydrock, Cornwall, looking through to the kitchen beyond, was used for washing and cleaning. On the slate slab on the left kitchen pots were cleaned under steam. The 19th-century architect Roger Kerr described the Victorian country house kitchen as 'a complicated laboratory'.*

This was true of the handsome and compact little manor house of Nether Lyppiatt in Gloucestershire, *c.* 1705; as well as John Vanbrugh's glorious Seaton Delaval Hall in Northumberland, where the massive kitchen wing was balanced by that of the stable wing on the other side of the front court.

The separation of the kitchen from the house was not for purely architectural reasons but rather for practical purposes. It was considered important to keep the smells of the kitchen separate from the main house (an obsession of Victorian country house architects) and perhaps safer (in theory at least) to keep the continuous fires of the kitchen separate from the main residential block. To modern eyes, however, it can seem extraordinary that steaming food passed through cold outside courtyards before arriving on the table.

While many great historic kitchens in today's country houses survive from the eighteenth century, the technology seen in them usually dates from rather later, from late nineteenth- or early twentieth-century refittings, such as the massive cast-iron ranges with their separate oven spaces and a warren of supporting rooms, pantries, larders and laundries.

THE VICTORIAN KITCHEN: A WELL-OILED MACHINE

THE NINETEENTH-CENTURY kitchen proper was used for cooking, while all forms of wet or dirty work in the cleaning or preparing of food took place in the scullery. The buttery remained the domain of the butler, where the silver and glass were cleaned. It was also usually where the plate safe (for silver) was located, along with the butler's bedroom for added security.

The mid-Victorian country house kitchen was described by the architect Robert Kerr in his *The Gentleman's House* (1864) as like a 'complicated laboratory'. Kerr's own book gave a great deal of advice on how to plan a kitchen, recommending that it should be not less than 18ft (5.5m) or 20ft (6m) by 25 (7.75m) or 30ft (9m), and he encouraged attention to detail when building a scullery: 'drainage is important for the vapours of the scullery drain are notably unpleasant'.

RIGHT: *The handsome 1760s Georgian stalls at Seaton
Delaval, Northumberland, are preserved in the hugely
impressive interior of the stable wing built earlier in the
century to designs by John Vanbrugh. They give a good
flavour of the grandeur of the Georgian stablewing; indeed,
the horse played a key role in the life, transport and
pleasure of the 19th- and early 20th-century country house.*

Stables: The Heart of a Country House?

ONE CANNOT ESCAPE the presence of the stable in the English country house. Essential for travel, the hunt and the racecourse, horses were central to the aristocratic way of life. Sir Osbert Sitwell observed of the horses in London in the early 1900s: 'Horses – horses and carriages more than people – gave London, as I remember it then, its particular distinction, for it was the capital of an island where the horse was still god, where stables were often finer than the house, racecourses better than the parks.'

The writer Daniel Defoe noted in *A Tour thro' Great Britain* (1724) that the seventeenth-century stables at Petworth (then demolished) were 'the first of their kind in Europe and equal to some noblemen's houses'.

Certainly from the late seventeenth century onwards stables often took on the style of the country house, sometimes appearing like a scaled-down version of the house. Indeed the eighteenth-century stables at Bowood House in Wiltshire were so grand that they were converted into the home of the Marquess of Lansdowne when the main house was demolished after World War II. The current house is so elegant that not a few visitors might be surprised to learn that it was once a stable.

The elegance of the stables was an extension of aristocratic display. Two wonderful examples of seventeenth-century stables survive with highly decorated stalls, handsome carved arches and original hay racks: one being at Whitmore Hall in Staffordshire, the other at Peover Hall in Cheshire. Both illustrate the quality of workmanship that was once lavished on stables. Another beautifully preserved example of a later eighteenth-century stable interior is that built within the earlier stable wing at Seaton Delaval in Northumberland.

Whereas the earlier stable blocks, as at Audley End, *c.* 1603, were principally long rectangular blocks, by the early eighteenth century the typical form for a stableyard was a stately quadrangle. From then on, quandrangle stables became a familiar and important feature of the topography. Handsome examples include Roger Morris' elegant Palladian stables at Althorp, designed *c.* 1730s, and the stables at Chatsworth, *c.* 1750s, designed by James

Paine, typifying a form encountered in many country houses. In some contexts, paired stable yards were built, as at Temple Newsam in Yorkshire, one serving as a stable and coachyard, the other as a riding school.

A typical Georgian quadrangle includes vaulted stables with accommodation for horses in stalls, as well as houses for coaches, along with rooms for storing tack and for lodging grooms and stable boys. The entrance was often marked by a cupola, carrying a clock. Servants' lodgings were commonly arranged on the upper floor, partly for reasons of security, as good horses were immensely valuable. Some country house stableyards also had kennels for fox hounds.

The great country house stables of the nineteenth century varied in style, some might be Gothic Revival (as at Scarisbrick Hall, *c.* 1860s, designed by A. W. N. Pugin); or Old English (as at Eaton Hall in Cheshire, *c.* 1870s, by Alfred Waterhouse); or Classical (as at Wimpole Hall,

RIGHT: *Whitmore Hall, Staffordshire, has one of the finest surviving early 17th-century stables in the country. Its stalls are separated by handsome carved columns, showing how stables were both functional and aesthetic.*

BELOW: *The Classical, early Georgian stable quadrangle at Althorp, Northamptonshire, designed by Roger Morris in the 1720s. From this date onwards, stables of large country houses were usually arranged as quadrangles.*

near Cambridge, *c.* 1850s by H. E. Kendall). Whatever their style, most stables retained the quadrangular form. For serious stable enthusiasts it is interesting to note that the royal Horseguards stables, *c*, 1750s, retain the exact use for which they were designed, as do John Nash's stables in the Royal Mews at Buckingham Palace (where 30 Windsor Grey and Cleveland Bay horses are kept alongside working coaches and can be visited by the public).

The mid-nineteenth-century stable block at Wimpole Hall (owned by the National Trust) illustrates as well as any how adaptable stable ranges can be for modern needs in a country house open to the public, including facilities such as shops, cafés and loos, while still retaining some stables for their original use.

CHAPTER SEVEN
READING THE CONTENTS

A Population of Portraits

THE PORTRAIT APPEARS everywhere in the country house interior. In a home that has passed down many generations, portraits play a significant role in telling the story of the house and its family, offering vital human clues that can be read alongside the evidence of the architecture and furnishings, adding an extra layer of understanding. The people portrayed on the walls of a long gallery, or along a deep staircase, are often the people who once lived in the house, shaped its designs and styles, chose its furnishings, collected its fine Italian sculpture and brought back battered arms from military expeditions overseas.

Costume, jewellery and armour all play a critical part in a portrait, revealing much about the person portrayed, the type of character he or she would have struck when moving through the handsome family house. Look at the richly detailed clothes of an Elizabethan nobleman, for instance, and imagine him walking past one of the ornate carved screens or tapestries of his Elizabethan manor. In the grand mansions of later periods, such as Wilton or Boughton, imagine how vividly the hostess's bristling, lustrous silks would have stood out in those marble halls.

RIGHT: *Hanging in the great hall at Berkeley Castle, Gloucestershire, the portrait of Lord Hunsdon (1591) shows but one of many generations of Berkeley ancestors and connections. At the opposite end of the hall hangs a portrait by William Gainsborough depicting Lord Hunsdon's descendant Admiral Sir George Berkeley.*

Portraits also usually reveal something of the family's political ideals and allegiances. The busts of the eighteenth-century Tory and Whig politicians, Charles James Fox and William Pitt, for instance, often appear in the halls of country houses, reflecting the family's loyalties and ideals. An unusual example, the Bishop of Durham's long gallery at Auckland Castle, *c.* 1550s, was hung with portraits of the great Protestant Reformers, such as Martin Luther, Thomas Cranmer and Hugh Latimer – definitely a case of hero worship.

TALKING HEADS: PORTRAITS AS DISPLAY

BEFORE THE sixteenth century there was very little in the way of portraiture as we know it today. The nearest equivalents were funerary monuments, but there were few 'movable' paintings or sculptures until the Tudor age, when the portrait became as much a part of the display of the family's importance and achievements as heraldry. Indeed many sixteenth- and early seventeenth-century portraits bear the family's coat of arms within the painting.

Portraits speak to us directly of a sitter's status, alliances and influence. Long galleries, such as the one at Hardwick, and many a country house staircase hung with portraits, such as that at Althorp, effectively provide a family tree in pictorial form. Such portraits were clearly intended to impress and inspire contemporary and future generations. In interiors, such as the dining or drawing room, painted portraits could have the same effect.

The full-length portrait was facilitated by the introduction of canvas in England during the last decades of the sixteenth century, and was part of the love of display so apparent in the architecture of the period. Full-length portraits suited the elevated architectural spaces of the sixteenth-century long gallery.

A fine set of full-lengths showing different members of the Sidney family can be seen at Penshurst Place in Kent, and an important collection (originally from Charlton Park in Wiltshire) can now be seen at Kenwood House in Middlesex. The best private portrait collection formed in the twentieth century is that at Parham House in Sussex where some outstanding examples can be seen in the late sixteenth-century house, restored by the Pearson family in the 1920s.

RIGHT: *The full-length portraits on the staircase at the Treasurer's House in York (restored by collector Frank Green in the 1890s and left by him to the National Trust) show the consistent scale of grand portraiture during the 17th and 18th centuries and the gestures and postures reminiscent of Classical sculpture.*

Elizabethan and Jacobean court and gentry were also great commissioners of the miniature, but these were for private contemplation rather than public display and were stored in cases like precious gems, rather than on a wall. While portraits of monarchs and admired contemporaries would be displayed in halls and long galleries – essentially the public rooms of parade – the more intimate portraits of friends and family more often appeared in family quarters or cabinets.

A PATTERN OF GLAMOUR: FROM VAN DYCK TO KNELLER

AN EYE TO FUTURE opinion was shown by the Countess of Sussex, when, on choosing the costume for her portrait by Anthony van Dyck, she noted: 'too rich in jewels I am sure, but 'tis no great matter for another age to think me richer than I was'.

Portraits also came to be treated as heirlooms that passed on with the other fixtures and main house of an estate, while the more movable furniture could be left to other descendants and dependants. From the eighteenth century it became quite common for relations to commission copies of the original portraits retained with the estate. By the nineteenth century portrait copying had become quite big business.

Court portrait painters (many of whom came from the Netherlands) tended to set the fashion and were patronized by the great nobility, while the gentry found worthy imitators, such as Gilbert Jackson. No one in the history of English portraiture has rivalled Anthony van Dyck's rich but refined and elegant portrait style. Van Dyck's evocative images of the court and courtiers of Charles I, clad in lustrous silks and lace, displaying an intelligent, well-bred, nonchalant air, set a pattern in portraiture for at least 200 years. Fine examples include the beautiful portrait of the Countess of Bedford at Petworth House in Sussex, or the vast and stately group portrait of the Earl of Pembroke and his family at Wilton, in which the earl and his countess, dressed in black, sit before an armorial hanging, surrounded by the young clad in highly coloured silks.

During the Restoration, Charles II's principal portrait painter was Sir Peter Lely whose work can be seen in numerous country houses, including Ham House in Surrey. It is worth noting, however, that not even the great painters undertook the whole execution of a portrait, but

rather relied on assistants. Van Dyck certainly used drapery painters, as did Lely. Godfrey Kneller (court portrait painter to five monarchs, from Charles II to George I) ran something of a factory, with assistants specializing in landscape, clothes and hands. Kneller is said to have observed that he had: '14 persons sit to him in a day'. Kneller's studio was responsible for thousands of paintings, and his style was also much imitated by provincial painters. The publicity did him no harm though. A wealthy man, he was made baronet in 1715. As in the Tudor period, royal Stuart and Hanoverian portraits were much reproduced in country houses of the period, without necessarily implying a direct royal connection.

How the finished portrait was hung in country houses at this time is suggested by a remark in Samuel Pepys' *Diary* on 7 September 1665 during a visit to Swakeley's in Middlesex: 'Pretty to see over the skreene of the hall … the King's Head, and my Lord of Essex on one side, and Fairfax on the other; upon the other side of the Skreene, the parson of the parish, and the lord of the manor and his sisters.'

Georgian portraiture: a golden age

The eighteenth century, which is often regarded as the golden age of British portraiture, produced diverse portraits, ranging from grandly posed individuals to touching family groups, who are liberally represented throughout the country houses of England. The towering figure of the age and leading painter of the period was certainly Sir Joshua Reynolds, who did more than any other artist to assert the professional status of the painter. First President of the Royal Academy of Arts, Reynolds was also portrait painter to King George III, although he referred to himself as 'of near equal dignity with His Majesty's rat catcher'. King George himself preferred Allan Ramsay (who had trained in Italy).

Reynolds, who, like his contemporary William Hogarth, believed in putting some psychological insight into a portrait, moved away from the formalistic, icon-like qualities of traditional portraiture to create something more human and personal, particularly in his group portraits of families, children and friends, known as conversation pieces. Reynolds was also a practical man and he once wrote to a client in 1777: 'a portrait requires three sittings about an hour and a half each time but, if the sitter chooses it, the face could be finished in one day'.

Some society portrait painters, such as Philippe Mercier, settled in fashionable towns and cities, such as York, which had a lively season with races and balls. Thomas Gainsborough resided for a long time in Bath, the popular spa of the eighteenth and early nineteenth centuries. The great 'swagger' portraitist of his day, Gainsborough portrayed his sitters with a becoming, aristocratically nonchalant swagger. So successful was his portrait business, that he once wrote: 'I'm sick of Portraits and wish to take my viol da Gamba and walk off to some sweet Village where I can paint Landskips and to enjoy the fag end of life in quietness and ease.'

Many of Gainsborough's best pictures do, indeed, show landowning couples sitting in landscapes, such as *Mr and Mrs Browne of Tunstall, c*. 1755, at Houghton Hall, Norfolk, or his particularly famous *Mr and Mrs Robert Andrews, c*. 1748–9 (now in the National Portrait Gallery), in which Mr Andrews, accompanied by his wife and dog, is shown leaning nonchalantly against a tree, shotgun under his arm, as he surveys the landscape. Gainsborough's last words are said to have been 'we are all going to heaven and Van Dyck is of the company'. The equestrian portraits of George Stubbs are some of the most memorable images of English aristocratic life; these include *The Milbanke and Melbourne Families*, now in the National Gallery, London.

Throughout the eighteenth century the Grand Tour occupied young noblemen and gentlemen of fortune who spent a few years travelling in Europe, particularly in Italy, as part of their education (see page 140). Thus quite a healthy business grew up with portrait painters recording the young English *milordi* often pictured with their tutors by some fine Classical ruin or antique bust or vase, such as *Lord Warkworth*, 1763, by Nathaniel Dance, depicting the young Warkworth with his tutor at Rome (now at Syon House).

Pompei Batoni, one of the popular Rome-based artists, essentially provided the Grand Tourist with a very grand holiday snap. Other notable artists based in Rome included Anton Mengs and Angelica Kauffman.

RIGHT: *At Renishaw Hall, Derbyshire, hangs one of the finest group portraits produced by John Singer Sargent, showing Sir George Sitwell and his family. His son, Osbert, observed in his memoir,* Left Hand, Right Hand! *(1945): 'in order to make a living in England during the late Victorian and the Edwardian ages every portrait painter had, to a certain extent, become a faker of old masters'. To this English practice, Sargent added a dash of French Impressionism.*

Sir Thomas Lawrence was the great portrait painter of the early nineteenth century. His most famous works include *Arthur Wellesley, 1st Duke of Wellington, c.* 1814, and the other allied sovereigns and commanders at Waterloo which hang in the Waterloo Chamber at Windsor Castle. Like most of the great portraitists, Lawrence continued to paint on the scales set by the Jacobean full-length as well as the half-length, depending on the requirements of the rooms for which he was painting. His contemporary, George Richmond, painted portraits of great sensitivity in oils, watercolour and chalk.

NEW OLD MASTERS: VICTORIAN AND EDWARDIAN DAUBS

THE GREAT VICTORIAN PAINTERS include John Everett Millais, a president of the Royal Academy and founder of the Pre-Raphaelite Brotherhood; and Edwin Landseer, who painted major sporting portraits of family groups on gruesome-looking stalking trips to Scotland. J. F. Herring produced many fine sporting images; and Sir Francis Grant turned out numerous hunting scenes. Indeed the British gent being such a sporting-mad creature in the main, it is unsurprising that in not a few houses the portraits of racehorses seem of rather better quality than the portraits of people. But the reverse could also be true, as Henry James once observed in a letter from Eggesford House in Devon in 1878: 'There is nothing in the house but pictures of horses and awfully bad ones.'

Given the wealth produced by British commerce and industry at the turn of the twentieth century, it is no surprise that English portraiture was highly regarded by the art world. The British aristocracy adopted the brilliant American-born John Singer Sargent, whose languid depictions of an unnaturally handsome aristocracy still colour our perception of that world. Examples range from the brilliant, shining grandeur of the Duke and Duchess of Marlborough in *The Marlborough Family* (1905) at Blenheim, to the still beauty of *The Countess of Rocksavage* (1922), which hangs at Houghton.

The writer Sir Osbert Sitwell has left a charming record in *Left Hand, Right Hand!* (1945) of the family's sitting for Sargent. The family portrait, which now hangs at Renishaw Hall in

Derbyshire, depicts the Sitwells on their landed property, aristocratic in pose but informally grouped. Sitwell's account gives a good insight into the spur behind, and process of portrait-commissioning by a landed family at the turn of the last century.

By the end of the nineteenth century, photographs appeared in profusion in most country houses, as part of the tradition of marking status and connections. In the homes of titled families, it is worth keeping an eye out for the signed photographs of royalty, made fashionable by Edward VII and his daughter-in-law, Queen Mary. Royal photographs are often accompanied by photographs of family members clad in the ceremonial robes worn for state occasions, such as the coronation, or the opening of parliament. Other family photos might be formal engagement or debutante portraits.

The portrait collections of country houses still in the hands of the family might include more recently commissioned works, such as the Lucian Freud portraits at Chatsworth House; or Paul Benney's *Sir Reresby and Lady Sitwell* (1995) at Renishaw Hall in Derbyshire; also Andrew Festing's remarkable group portraits of the staff of the past decade at Holkham Hall. Good portraits have also been commissioned by the Foundation for Art who support the work of the National Trust, for example, Binny Mathews' portrait of Julius Drewe, the last member of the Drewe family to live at Castle Drogo in Devon.

2. Moving Furniture

FURNITURE IS BY nature mostly movable. The term 'movables' generally refers to possessions that can be packed up and taken from house to house. More technically, 'movable' can also mean furniture and other items that, legally, can be left in specific bequests to individual members of a family while the main estate, including mansion and title plus nominated portraits, passed down the line.

Furnishing a country house was usually spurred on by the twin desires for comfort and impressive display. In this country many interesting pieces of furniture, crafted by the great furniture-makers, particularly from the eighteenth and nineteenth centuries, remain in their original context, giving us a further insight into these periods. But a note of caution should be sounded, as not all historical furnishings necessarily originated in the houses they are now in; some period pieces might have been acquired to enhance an interior designed in an 'Old English' style, a common practice during the nineteenth and early twentieth centuries, with the fashion for recapturing the past. Period collections of arms, for instance, were often acquired later.

Very little furniture survives *in situ* from the pre-Tudor age. The earliest-known chair, the coronation chair now at Westminster Abbey, was made for Edward I by one Walter of Durham in 1272. The earliest examples of furniture that can be matched to original inventories (i.e. survey lists of contents) are found at Hardwick Hall in Derbyshire.

On country house furniture, William Harrison commented in his *Description of England* (1577):

> The furniture of our houses also exceedeth and is grown in manner even to passing delicacy... in noblemen's houses it is not rare to see an abundance of arras, rich hangings of tapestry, silver vessel, and so much other plate as may furnish sundry cupboards, to the sum oftentimes of £1,000 and £2,000 at least.

Harrison also described in the homes of knights, gentlemen and merchants 'great provision of tapestry, turkeywork, pewter brass'.

A fair amount of Tudor oak furniture dating from the sixteenth century does survive and is a familiar sight in country houses. Examples include chests made up of panelled construction with linenfold panelling (see page 104); buffet cupboards with chunky, bulbous posts, and either open shelves, if an early example, or closed doors, if later; substantial framed and carved beds (with panelled headboards and bulbous posts), as well as stools and chairs.

RIGHT: *The state bed at Dyrham Park, Gloucestershire, c. 1700, belongs to the golden age of upholstery in English furniture. The rich velvets were all carefully chosen to play their part in the sense of progress that underpinned the Baroque apartment system.*

Today we are accustomed to seeing such Tudor furniture out on display, highly polished and treasured for evidence of craftsmanship and for the texture of dark, old oak (which was much admired, imitated and even faked in the nineteenth century). But in the Tudor period, such furniture would usually have been presented against tapestry and covered with bright textiles. The conventional lid-chest provided the principal storage in a room, as well as its seating. Early benches, indeed, often combined a chest with back and arms. During the sixteenth century the panelled sides of chests were reduced, and the frames exposed as legs connected by stretchers.

THE ARRIVAL OF THE CABINET-MAKERS

JACOBEAN FURNITURE SHARED many characteristics with Tudor pieces, but had more delicate inlay in holly and elm woods, and evolved in a variety of ways. The chest of drawers, for instance, had by mid-century replaced the lid-chest as the principal storage space.

Tudor tables had often been essentially trestle tables, capable of being entirely dismantled, but in the seventeenth century draw-tables were developed that could be extended in length, although still usually with large bulbous legs. The oval-topped gate-leg table was developed later in the seventeenth century, on shapely turned legs (on which the decorative quality was achieved by being turned on a lathe).

The late seventeenth century saw the emergence of the skilled cabinetmaker as an independent figure in the marketplace, a development stimulated by the influx of Huguenot (Protestant) refugees from France and the Low Countries after 1685. Walnut became the most admired and cherished wood for furniture, and great decorative effect was made of the elaborate grain of the wood. Also popular were lacquered and 'Japanned' cabinets, characterized by pale, gilt and oriental decoration on a dark or dark red background. Marquetry, a style of ornate inlaid woodwork, was also fashionable.

Substantially upholstered furniture, such as chairs and stools, first developed during the seventeenth century, stools appearing as early as *c.* 1600. It was also the age of extravagant bed

LEFT: *William Kent's 1720s design of tables and pier-glasses (with tall mirrors between windows) at Houghton Hall, Norfolk, creates a strongly architectural effect. Houghton has one of the best-preserved sequences of early 18th-century interiors in England.*

upholstery, with dizzyingly high overhanging roofs (known as testers) and hangings. Such grand state beds were usually placed in the principal room of a great apartment, where the bed's lush upholstery – all gilding and richness of textile and texture – helped to build up the prestige of the room's occupant and answered the sense of expectation experienced by visitors progressing through the great apartment towards the privileged bedchamber. A fine example of rich bed upholstery can be seen in the Venetian Ambassador's Room at Knole in Kent and at Dyrham Park in Gloucestershire. Chairbacks also became notably taller during the period.

From around 1700 cabinets were often set up high on stands of handsomely turned legs, joined by cross-pieces. In the early years of the century the cabriole leg appeared, which curves outwards at the knee and tapers inwards below. The cabriole initially terminated first in a club or pad foot, but from 1710 to 1750, the claw and ball became more typical. Early on in the century mahogany, imported from the West Indies, became the most popular wood for furniture, as it did not warp as easily as other woods and could be beautifully carved.

During the 1720s and 30s, furniture took on a more architectural quality, exemplified by the grand state beds and also by the tall bureau cabinets, often pedimented, with a cupboard or bookcase over a fold-down desk. William Kent's furniture for great houses, such as Houghton and Wilton, was strongly architectural in character, as can be seen in the side-tables and mirrors. Kent's side-tables are very distinctive, with large scrolled and gilded bases supporting marble tops, often decorated with shells, masks and eagles. Note also how the tall, heavily framed and gilded mirrors at Houghton create an architectural rhythm.

GEORGIAN CABINET-MAKERS

IN THE EIGHTEENTH CENTURY leading London craftsmen often supplied country houses: the cabinet-maker William Hallet, for instance, worked at Badminton; William Vile and John Cobb produced furniture for Sir Mathew Fetherstonhaugh at Uppark in Sussex; Matthew Lock supplied Hinton House in Somerset (this work is now in the Victoria and Albert Museum); while Channon & Grendley produced pieces for Kedleston Hall in Derbyshire.

RIGHT: *The comfortable library at Tatton Park, Cheshire, is a classic example of a well-furnished Regency interior, with useful chairs and sofa reflecting a new expectation of comfort; the furniture was supplied by Gillows of Lancaster.*

As in architecture, pattern books had a critical influence on furniture of the period. The publication of the leading cabinet-maker Thomas Chippendale's *Gentleman and Cabinet-maker's Director* (1754) advertised his furniture to patrons and influenced other makers, both in London and the provinces. Indeed provincial cabinet-makers clearly copied original pieces of furniture as well as designs from the *Director*.

The *Director* made Chippendale one of the best-known furniture designers of the age (perhaps any age) and his name most misleadingly became almost a byword for mid-eighteenth century furniture, for the glazed front bookcase and ribbon-backed dining chair. Chippendale designs ranged from fanciful chinoiserie to the light-hearted Gothic of the 1750s and 1760s. A set of very handsome furniture of this character, made by William Hallett, remains *in situ* in the picture gallery in Temple Newsam near Leeds.

The Universal System of Household Furniture (1762), produced by the cabinet-makers William Ince and John Mayhew, provided another important pattern source. For furniture in the Gothic style there was Batty Langley's *Specimens of Ancient Carpentry* (1740).

A CYCLE OF REVIVALS

FROM THE 1760s, partly under the influence of Adam's furnishings for great houses, furniture took on a newly refined quality. Designing his suites in a spirit of deliberate delicacy derived from classical decoration, Adam said he wanted 'to transfuse the beautiful spirit of antiquity with novelty and variety'.

Adam's interiors at Harewood House in Yorkshire still show many fine examples of furniture made to his designs by Thomas Chippendale, as does the saloon at Saltram in Devon. In grand saloons and dining rooms Adam seems to have initiated the grand sideboard, a form of specially designed side-table, accompanied by pedestals on either side for storage. George Hepplewhite's *Cabinet-maker and Upholsterer's Guide* (1788) and Thomas Sheraton's *The Cabinet Maker's and Upholsterer's Drawing Book* (1791–4) helped to popularize the Adam style around the country.

Around 1800, there is a noticeable move away from the almost exaggerated delicacy of Adam's influence (denigrated by Horace Walpole as reminiscent of 'gingerbread and snippets of embroidery') towards something more monumental and overtly neo-Classical in furniture design.

Furniture of the Regency era (loosely 1800–30) accounts for a lot of the solid, rather masculine pieces sometimes seen in dining rooms and libraries today (from Ickworth House in Suffolk to Goodwood House in Sussex). One of the major Regency influences was Thomas Hope's *Household Furniture and Interior Decoration* (1807), which helped to circulate designs inspired by a new understanding of Greek style, sometimes referred to as 'Empire style' as it coincided with the style for furniture under Napoleon's imperial phase. Hope was himself a wealthy collector who had first designed Greek-style furniture to complement his own collection of antiquities.

The Regency was a period of pared-down Classical details, such as plain Doric columns, vase-like or lyre-shapes for chairs. It was also a period of darker woods and the widespread use of darker veneers, such as rosewood and amboyna, outlined in brass with neo-Classical patterns. One of the leading designers of the Regency was Gillows of Lancaster whose furniture can be seen in a number of houses, including Tatton Park in Cheshire and Uppark in Sussex.

After the defeat of Napoleon in 1815, when travel to France resumed, there was a revival of interest in the French style of Louis XV and XVI, as exemplified in the furnishing of the Elizabeth Saloon at Belvoir Castle in Rutland. The Prince Regent admired *boulle*, a luxurious form of veneer, named after the French furniture-maker André-Charles Boulle who supplied Louis XIV. *Boulle* work consists of ornate surfaces decorated in tortoise shell inlaid with bronze.

In England *boulle* work was associated with the workshop of George Bullock, who also specialized in robust Gothic Revival furniture. The cabinet-makers Nicholas Morel and George Seddon supplied a large amount of ornate, French-inspired furnishing for Windsor Castle and many other country houses.

From the 1830s onwards, a huge variety of styles and sources emerged, offering enormous scope to the nineteenth-century patron and furniture-maker. J. C. Loudon listed the styles of the 1830s in *An Encyclopedia of Cottage, Farm and Villa Architecture and Furniture* (1835) as: 'Grecian, Gothic or perpendicular, Elizabethan or Louis XIV'. A. W. N. Pugin (who designed

LEFT: *The 'Sussex'-style bench at Wightwick Manor,*
Staffordshire, is typical of the work of Morris & Co
which took its inspiration from the good old honest
workmanship of local craftsmen, rather than aristocratic
or Classical precedents.

READING
THE CONTENTS

all the furniture and fittings for the Palace of Westminster when it was rebuilt in the 1840s) championed the medieval, but sought for a purer approach, away from what seemed like the frivolity of eighteenth-century Rococo Gothic.

Sir Walter Scott, whose novels popularized a Romantic view of the past, furnished his baronial-style home Abbotsford in Scotland with Tudor- and Elizabethan-style pieces by George Bullock. In 1828 Scott had observed of the substantial furniture of his age: 'An ordinary chair, in the most ordinary parlour has now something of Grecian massiveness at once, and elegance in its forms. That of twenty or thirty years since was mounted on four tapering and tottering legs, resembling four tobacco pipes.'

Much of the more florid Victorian furniture commonly associated with the Victorian era stems from a Rococo Revival, recapturing the style of Louis XV, which became very popular in the mid-nineteenth century. The Rococo Revival also coincided with the innovation of coil-sprung armchairs. The ornate French style of the Victorian era is shown at its most lavish at Baron Ferdinand de Rothschild's Waddesdon Manor in Buckinghamshire.

In a reaction to mass-produced furniture, William Morris and Philip Webb championed the skills of the vernacular craftsman, inspiring the Arts and Crafts movement, which was very influential in country houses, despite its decidedly non-aristocratic approach. Morris himself set up a company to manufacture and supply well-designed furniture, of which the rush-seated Sussex chair is the most familiar reminder. Morris & Co furnished and decorated a number of major country houses, including Wightwick Manor, near Wolverhampton, in 1887.

The 1870s also saw a new fashion develop, inspired by the simpler, lighter furniture of traditional Japanese design. The style was associated with the Aesthetic Movement and the interiors of houses designed by E. W. Godwin, such as the Chelsea home of Oscar Wilde.

One of the defining features of house furnishing during the early years of the twentieth century was the rise in the taste for collecting antiques, and furnishing houses with pieces from the correct period, whereas formerly each generation had added pieces in the style of the age. Although some interest in such antiquarianism developed in the mid-nineteenth century, the approach did

RIGHT: *The rare, recently restored
1930s interior, designed for Sam
Courtauld at Eltham Palace,
Middlesex, provides one of the few
examples of early 20th-century
progressive taste that can be
appreciated in something like
its original form today.*

not affect the majority of furnishings until the early twentieth century, when examples could be
seen in *Country Life* photographs, such as Avebury Manor, Wiltshire.

The Treasurers' House in York exemplifies the antiquarian approach, with a wide range of
period furniture, which was collected at the turn of the century, specifically for the different
periods represented throughout the house's interior. The Treasurer's House set a pattern of
furnishing informed by a modern sense of period appropriateness and historical context.

In the past twenty years, the emphasis in collecting and furnishing has been on finding the most attractive and comfortable way to present older pieces, as can be seen at Althorp in Northamptonshire and Goodwood in Sussex. New one-off items of furniture are today occasionally commissioned by country house owners, but it is rare for a whole room set to be commissioned or acquired afresh. Instead, modern touches usually emerge through the addition of contemporary art, particularly sculpture and ceramics, as can be seen at Stonor Park in Oxfordshire.

LEFT: *Painshill Park, Surrey, illustrates the contrived landscape garden of the mid-18th century with contrasting plantings and buildings, creating different moods for the delight of the visitor. After years of neglect, Painshill has recently been restored.*

CHAPTER EIGHT
READING THE GARDEN

The Joy of Gardening

To THE MODERN EYE, the country house and its garden seem almost indivisible, and many who visit country houses today go to enjoy the gardens as much as the buildings. Sharing the national delight in gardens, the Elizabethan philosopher Francis Bacon observed in *Of Gardens* (1597) that he regarded gardening 'as the purest of humane pleasures; without which, Buildings and Pallaces are but Grosse Handy-works'. The joys of gardening, and visiting gardens, however, can change dramatically with the seasons in a way that visiting houses perhaps does not.

Just as architecture reflects changes in taste and patterns of social behaviour, so does garden design, as I hope to show in this chapter. In the first section, I will give a brief overview of early formal country house gardens – of which there are few real survivors – that preceded the great landscape movement of the eighteenth century. I also want to look at that great revolution in taste itself, the landscape park with its attendant Arcadian world of Classical statues and temples, which can still be encountered in many fine gardens, from Chatsworth to Burghley

RIGHT: *One of the ornate banqueting houses at Campden House, Chipping Campden in Gloucestershire. The formal gardens of the late 16th and early 17th century often contained such delightful banqueting houses where guests would enjoy a pudding course within sight and smell of the plants that lay sugared and decorated on their plates.*

and Blenheim, and which influenced taste across Europe and America. Finally I would like to show how garden design in the nineteenth and twentieth centuries, which has informed so much of what we see today, was in some way inspired by an active sense of the beauties of the past.

The relationship of the garden to the medieval country house was governed by utility. The earliest recorded English gardens were often associated with convents and royal palaces. In the 1090s, William Rufus recorded a visit to the Benedictine Abbey at Romsey in Hampshire where he saw a garden of herbs and roses. Above all roses were cherished both for their nourishing qualities and fragrance, as well as for their symbolic connection to the Virgin Mary. Herbs, by contrast, were used for cooking and medicines.

EXOTIC ENCLOSURES: TUDOR AND STUART GARDENS

EARLY TUDOR GARDENS were probably arranged in enclosed courtyards – sometimes known as the 'hortus conclusus'. In royal palaces, such as Windsor under Henry III, these fragrant courts were designed to be seen and enjoyed from elevated and covered walks and galleries. They often contained fountains framed by intricate knot gardens of evergreen plants, such as rosemary and hyssop. The knot design also had philosophical overtones symbolizing the unending line – and thus infinity.

Tudor gardens were designed for pleasure as well as utility. Knot gardens reached a pitch of elegance and colourful contrivance in the mid-sixteenth century – one of the finest in the country can be seeen at Thornbury Castle in Gloucestershire. Knot gardens were often interspersed with areas of lawn, fountains and carved heraldic beasts, which were known to have stood in the great privy garden at Hampton Court. Tunnel-like arbours were also planted with roses and grass, creating pleasant shaded and scented walks, as well as bowling greens.

Typical plants were likely to be natives, such as cornflowers and heartsease. But the sixteenth century was also an era of exploration and enthusiasm for exotic seeds and plants, such as gentians and cyclamen, prized for their rarity and novelty, which were brought back from all over Europe

and the New World. As William Harrison wrote in *The Description of England* (1577): 'It is a wonder to see how many strange herbs, plants and unusual fruits are daily brought unto us from the Indies, Americas, Taprobane, Canary Islands and all parts of the world.'

The sixteenth-century also saw the emergence of patterned parterres or beds, reflecting the popular passion for heraldry encouraged by the Tudor court. Thomas Hill's *The Profitable Art of Gardening* (1568) is filled with numerous designs for labyrinthine gardens, with patterned beds. Fortuitously, there were at the time a number of gifted professional gardeners who could lay out such gardens, such as the Tradescants of Lambeth, who worked at Hatfield House; and the Dutch gardener Mathias L'Obel (after whom Lobelia was named) advised on the gardens of Lord Zouche at Parham House in Sussex.

Most Elizabethan houses would have a flower garden laid out in the knot design, with walks and seats, situated on the south side, where it could be seen and enjoyed from the main rooms of the house and from the roof.

Banqueting houses became a feature of late Elizabethan and Jacobean country houses, such as Montacute and Campden House in Chipping Campden. These delightful little buildings were intended for use not just as garden picnic houses, but as places to indulge in the banquet, or pudding course of sugared confections, which was taken in a separate place from the main meal. Banqueting houses might be found on a roof or raised part of a terrace and they often seem to have overlooked the very gardens that probably supplied the fragrant delicacies for the table.

Leading fashionable taste in the Jacobean period, Queen Anne of Denmark and her eldest son, Prince Henry, both had their palace gardens (at Somerset House in Greenwich and Richmond) redesigned by the French garden architect Salomon de Caus in elaborate formal spaces with fountains, grottoes, automata and statues on top of columns. Salomon's younger brother, Isaac de Caus, created formal gardens in the same style at great courtiers' houses, such as Woburn Abbey in Bedfordshire and Wilton House in Wiltshire, where elements of the original survive today, namely the grotto-like banqueting house at Wilton and probably some of its great cedars.

Courtier Sir Henry Fanshawe had a garden at Ware Park in Hertfordshire, of which the historian William Campden wrote that there were 'none excelling it in flowers, physic herbs and fruit, in which things he did delight'. In 1606 Ware Park was laid out in a star pattern and then in 1616 given the water effects of the royal palaces. Inigo Jones was particularly conscious of the relationship between the house and its garden, and famously remodelled the gardens of Arundel House, the Duke of Norfolk's London residence, to display antique sculpture in the manner of an Italian Renaissance garden.

French taste was influential throughout the seventeenth century. The gardener André Mollet appeared in England before and after the Civil War designing *parterres de broderie*, or beds in the manner of embroidery, for Charles I's Queen, Henrietta Maria, at Wimbledon House. During the Restoration John Evelyn was an influential author and designer of formal gardens, not least at his family home of Wootton in Surrey.

The tall-windowed, south-facing orangery remained a popular feature in the seventeenth- and eighteenth-century garden, although oranges had first made an appearance as early as the late sixteenth century in aristocratic gardens. Samuel Pepys recorded in his *Diary* seeing the orange trees of Lord Brooke in June 1666: 'I pulled one off a little by stealth and eat it.'

LINES OF MAJESTY: THE LATE STUART GARDEN

THE STUART RESTORATION also saw the introduction of the French fashion for long canals and avenues of trees (or rides) linking elaborate gardens close to the house with the wider deer park and surrounding landscape. Great avenues were planted at this time at Boughton House in Northamptonshire and at Badminton in Gloucestershire. The great lines of trees, symbolizing the authority of man over nature, appear in the many topographical views of country houses set in their landscapes illustrated by the Dutch artists Johannes Kip and Leonard Knyff, and published in 1707 and 1715.

The same illustrations reveal that the gardens close to the house at this time were still prodigiously formal affairs, with clipped yews, gravel paths, pots, statues and fountains, as the

RIGHT: *Levens Hall, Cumbria, has a famous topiary garden that was initially laid out in around 1700 for Colonel James Grahame by a Frenchman called Beaumont. Restored in the early 19th century it is beautifully presented today, conjuring up the romance of an old garden, perhaps more than a formal one.*

diarist Celia Fiennes observed: 'exact uniform plots'. Recreations of such gardens can be seen at Ham House in Surrey and at Tredegar in Gwent. Levens Hall in Cumbria still has a formal topiary garden that was first laid out in the later seventeenth century, by one Guillaume Beaumont, the grid of which survives today, although it was much restored in the nineteenth century. The yews are now combined with very imaginative seasonal planting.

From the early eighteenth century, the evocation of the Classical world dominated fashionable garden design. The garden at Tottenham Park in Wiltshire, for instance, had a long broad sweep of lawn, terminating in a curve decorated with antique sculpture. The design, which was in line with the ancient writer Pliny's descriptions of Roman villas, reflected the new interest in Italian and antique exemplars which emerged from the popularity of the Grand Tour.

Moving Landscape

THE IDEALS OF THE Landscape movement that swept through garden designs of the period, aimed to combine Classical motifs, such as columns and temples, within a seemingly natural and pleasingly irregular landscape. One of the first garden designers to fully develop the idea of the contrived landscape was William Kent, one of the pivotal country house architects of the early-eighteenth-century Palladian movement. Horace Walpole wrote of his impact on gardening: 'He leaped the fence and saw that all nature was a garden.' Kent's view of landscape was influenced by his study of the major European landscape painters, such as Claude Lorrain and Salvador Rosa. In one of his first gardens, designed for Lord Burlington at Chiswick House, Kent planned the garden in informal, meandering walks, in which temples and columns formed the key vistas.

Both Stourhead in Warminster and Stowe in Buckinghamshire exemplify this tradition, with their sophisticated Arcadian landscapes of contrived natural beauty (both now ably cared for by the National Trust). Alexander Pope, for whom Kent also designed temples and whose own

RIGHT: *The expansive park at Blenheim Palace, Oxfordshire, was one of the major landscapes designed by Lancelot 'Capability' Brown during the mid-18th century. With two great lakes created on either side of John Vanbrugh's bridge, it was much admired by contemporaries, including Thomas Jefferson, who noted that the turf was especially mown every ten days.*

garden was influential, wrote that the success of gardening lay in 'the contrasts, the management of surprises, and the concealment of the bounds'. For the modern visitor it is worth remembering that while the statues and temples can be enjoyed on an immediate level, a guidebook will usually explain the significance of the choice of particular Classical deities.

Among the landscapes of the 1730s–50s, Painshill in Surrey is a fine example of the landscape garden. Created by the Hon. Charles Hamilton, Painshill contains an eclectic range of temples – Classical, Gothic, a Turkish tent, as well as a grotto opening onto the lake – with diverse historical allusions. Each area was planted to evoke different sensations and emotions. Hamilton is known to have imported conifers and other plants from North America. (The park had become an overgrown wilderness before its recent triumphant restoration.)

THE GEORGIAN LANDSCAPER: MR 'CAPABILITY' BROWN

LANCELOT BROWN BEGAN his working life at Stowe and became known as 'Capability', after his belief in the 'capabilities' of a place. Brown's genius was for the grand-scale transformation of a landscape with great sweeps of grass, the creation of great dams and lakes and the large-scale planting of appropriate trees. Blenheim remains one of the great examples of his work, although Brown designed many grand estates and his landscapes were widely imitated. Walpole, who admired Brown's landscapes, commented, 'every journey is made through a succession of pictures'.

Brown's type of landscaping coincided with the new popularity of hunting and shooting, and the enclosure of former common land. On the issue of the 'new' parkland, Walpole observed: '...the leading step to all that has followed' was the sunken fence (or the ha-ha), which allowed grazing cattle or deer to roam freely in the landscape without visible enclosure.

A reaction to Brown in the 1780s included the promotion of the 'Picturesque' landscape, which was wilder and more dramatic, with greater contrasts (associated with the writings of Richard Payne Knight and Uvedale Price), as exemplified by Payne Knight's own house, Downton Castle in Herefordshire.

One of the unsung heroes of the Picturesque movement was William Gilpin, Rector of Boldre in Hampshire, an amateur watercolourist who published books based on his travels 'in search of Picturesque beauty'. His ideas and publications were very popular in the later eighteenth century, when sketching and painting were valued as arts of cultivation.

REGENCY TO MODERN: REVIVALS AND INVENTIONS

BROWN WAS SUCCEEDED in influence by the designer Humphry Repton, who continued to provide artful Picturesque landscaping solutions, but also developed some degree of formal planting close to the house itself, and encouraged patrons to think of links between house and garden. Repton's ingenuity is exemplified at Woburn, about which he wrote in *Fragments* (1816) that his proposals had 'nowhere been so fully realized as at Woburn Abbey', where he rerouted the river, replanted the park, built a conservatory and created a private garden for the family.

By contrast, Repton's contemporary, J. C. Loudon, espoused the cause of the formal garden, believing that gardens should be clearly differentiated from nature. Rejecting the Picturesque ideal, Loudon advocated the 'gardenesque' instead.

LEFT: *The recently restord parterre at Waddesdon Manor in Buckinghamshire illustrates the Victorian fashion for shaped beds, planted with brightly coloured bedding plants typical of the labour-intensive gardens of the later 19th century.*

READING
THE GARDEN

The early to mid-nineteenth century saw a revival of interest in formal gardens, inspired by Renaissance designs, but also by a passion for a wide variety of historical periods, including a romanticized view of the Elizabethan age, which, in turn, meant a revival of formal *parterre* gardens. As *parterre* beds were planted out in bedding plants, the character of a garden could be changed by a continual rotation of different coloured plants.

The taste for collecting exotics, that is to say plants collected abroad or imported from other countries, also reached a peak in the nineteenth century and few gardens illustrate this better than Biddulph Grange Garden in Staffordshire.

Above all, the great Victorian gardens should be seen as pleasure gardens, designed for glamour and entertainment, for well-provisioned tea on the lawn and strolls from the house by the owner's family and guests.

The scale of conservatories and winter gardens reached a breathtaking scale during the nineteenth century, typified by Joseph Paxton's glasshouses at Chatsworth. Tatton Park in Cheshire has a handsome juxtaposition of an orangery by Lewis Wyatt and a fernery by Paxton, with ferns planted in a rocky setting.

FROM KITCHENS TO COTTAGES: THE ROMANCE OF GARDENING

THE NINETEENTH CENTURY was also the great age of the kitchen garden which supplied the needs of the household. Among the restored examples of nineteenth-century kitchen gardens is that at Felbrigg in Norfolk and Down House in Kent, the country home of Charles Darwin. Darwin was interested in the processes of gardening, but his gardener described Darwin in old age as '…moon[ing] about in the garden and I have seen him standing before a flower for ten minutes at a time. If he only had something to do I really believe he would do better.'

One of the best surviving examples of the taste for formal Italian-style gardens championed by the late nineteenth- and early twentieth-century architects Reginald Blomfield and Harold Peto flourishes at Renishaw Hall in Derbyshire. It was designed by the eccentric landowner Sir George Sitwell, Bt, with yew hedge enclosures framing views and vistas to carefully placed

RIGHT: *Great Dixter, Sussex, one of England's finest gardens, was laid out from 1910 by Nathaniel Lloyd with Edwin Lutyens and Gertrude Jekyll, around a restored 15th-century manor house, now the home of Nathaniel's son, gardens writer Christopher Lloyd.*

sculpture. Sir George had visited hundreds of Italian gardens and wrote *On the Making of Gardens* (1909).

At around the same time the most influential team of the early twentieth century who were to dominate fashionable garden design for many decades had come together in the form of Gertrude Jekyll and Edwin Lutyens. Jekyll drew her inspiration not from the great country house gardens of the past or from abroad, but from native cottage and farmhouse gardens.

From those gardens she reinvented the herbaceous border according to her late nineteenth-century artistic training, and reapplied it to country house gardens in different guises throughout the twentieth century. One of the most famous houses and gardens on which Jekyll and Lutyens collaborated was Great Dixter in Sussex, now the home of the gardens writer Christopher Lloyd.

Sissinghurst in Kent, where Vita Sackville-West and Harold Nicolson created their famous garden, illustrates the importance of blending garden design with architecture and the varied sensations created by different plantings. The garden of Lawrence Johnston at Hidcote was also among the more influential interwar gardens, famous for its richly planted enclosures, but described by Vita Sackville-West as 'a cottage garden on the most glorified scale'.

LATER TWENTIETH-CENTURY GARDENS: A CHANGING WORLD

THE MID-TWENTIETH CENTURY saw a radical shift in the fate of English country house gardens. Even before 1939 it was impossible to employ the numbers of staff that had been employed in the nineteenth-century garden. World War II had seen the grounds of a great number of gardens ploughed up or put to some alternative war use. For many owners the first priority in the aftermath of war was the preservation of their house and the economics of the estate.

The post-war years saw a reduction in the scale of ambitious garden management, although some famous gardens, such as those at Bodnant in Wales and Newby Hall in Yorkshire, have been maintained to the finest level throughout the century. One of the very few immediate post-war gardens of any real scale was designed by Sir Geoffrey Jellicoe for the royal family at Sandringham.

PREVIOUS PAGES: *The Privy Garden at Hampton Court Place, Surrey, was restored in 1991–6 to its original, late Stuart character, faithfully recapturing the shaped parterres that were originally laid out for William and Mary.*

RIGHT: *The garden at Little Sparta, Scotland, created by the poet Ian Hamilton-Findlay in an old farm in the Pentland Hills, captures with great skill the effect of contemporary sculpture or carved texts in a garden.*

Since the 1960s, however, interest in garden history and gardening has flourished. With it has grown an enthusiasm for garden restoration or the creation of gardens in a style sympathetic to the historic house they serve. This is shown at Parham House in Sussex where a fine flower garden has been created in the former kitchen garden to capture the same flavour of old England as represented by the house itself.

This intelligent and inventive modern attitude to the past is also shown in the recent work of the dowager Marchioness of Salisbury at Hatfield House in Hertfordshire, including a great knot garden. In similar spirit, the late Rosemary Verey of Barnsley House in Gloucestershire created a potager based on seventeenth-century kitchen garden plans. The Prince of Wales's garden at Highgrove House in Gloucestershire, where both the dowager Marchioness of Salisbury and Rosemary Verey advised, exemplifies the same gardening philosophy.

A parallel movement can be seen in the development of the National Trust's gardens under the stewardship of Graham Stuart-Thomas and John Sales, who aim to restore gardens, parks and kitchen gardens with a view to helping us understand the overall historic character of the house. The 1990s saw many magnificent historic garden restorations including the recreation of the Victorian *parterres* at Waddesdon Manor in Buckinghamshire, and the restoration of the 1690s Privy Garden at Hampton Court by Historic Royal Palaces.

In more recent times, a new and happy edge of hedonism has entered garden design, with gardens being created in which people can lose themselves in colour and contrast. Contributing to this movement is the fashion for placing modern sculpture in gardens and parks, as demonstrated at Antony House in Cornwall, at Saumarez Manor in Guernsey and at Burghley House in Lincolnshire. A related theme is the enjoyable water garden, such as the one recently created by Jacques and Peter Wirtz for the Duchess of Northumberland. In a similar spirit, the gardens at Alnwick Castle in Northumberland include sculptural fountains designed by William Pye.

Some of the most unusual garden designs of modern times are represented in the work of Charles Jencks in his own garden at Portrack near Dumfriess, and in the minimalist designs of Christopher Bradley-Hole, exemplified by his work at Bury Court in Hampshire.

236

Modern interests in planting areas in different grasses and perennials have been championed by Piet Oodoulf, who also designed the new garden at Scampston Hall in Yorkshire. The convergence of British plant connoisseurship and new approaches to layout has characterized the work of Tom Stuart-Smith at Windsor Castle.

Whatever you most enjoy when visiting a garden, it is always worth considering how a garden relates to the house it serves. Most importantly, consider which part of the garden would you most like to sit in for a whole day just to watch the changing effect of light on the patterns, enclosures and plants. Enjoy.

SELECTED PERIOD HOUSES

Period Houses at a Glance

S OME WELL- AND LESSER-KNOWN period houses have been selected to illustrate key aspects of the major architectural periods, spanning over 1000 years, and covering a wide range of styles and dwellings, from a Norman stronghold to an Edwardian recreation of a manor house. For a clearer understanding of period styles and building types, as well as technical architectural terms, see the brief stylistic guide and glossary at the end of the book, along with the suggested bibliography, which lists useful architectural histories and dictionaries.

COUNTRY HOUSE KEY

NT = National Trust

EH = English Heritage

HRP = Historic Royal Palaces

NOP = Not Open to the Public

LEFT: *Scarisbrick Hall, Lancashire, typifies the full-blooded Gothic Revival architecture of A. W. N. Pugin. This view shows the main entrance into the recreated Great Hall.*

EARLY PLANTAGENET (1154-1272)

HORTON COURT (NT)

Horton, nr Chipping Sodbury, Bristol BS17 6QR   Tel: 01985 843600

A late twelfth-century stone hall, probably built by Robert de Beaufeau, Prebendary of Salisbury Cathedral and Rector of Horton, with distinctive round-arched Norman windows and doors. It is one of the best survivals of the smaller manorial status house of the late Norman/early Plantagenet era.

CASTLE HEDINGHAM

Bayley Street, nr Halstead, Essex CO9 3DJ   Tel: 01787 460261

Built in 1184 by Aubrey de Vere, son of a knight in the service of William the Conqueror, Hedingham is one of the finest surviving Norman castles in England. Designed in the tradition of William I's Tower of London, it is tall and square with square corner towers.

LATER PLANTAGENET (1272-1399)

STOKESAY CASTLE (EH)

Stokesay, Craven Arms, Shropshire SY7 9AH   Tel: 01588 672544

A late thirteenth-century moated manor house, originally surrounded by a wall, Stokesay was built for the wealthy wool merchant Lawrence Ludlow, who had acquired the property in 1280. The great hall (which has a later roof) is lit by tall windows, and an external staircase leads to the first floor great chamber.

PENSHURST PLACE AND GARDENS

Penshurst, Kent TN11 8DG   Tel: 01892 870307

The great hall, dating back to the 1330s, was built for Sir John de Pulteney, a London merchant. It passed to Sir John Devereux who received a licence to crenellate in 1392, and built the walls and towers. An important medieval manor, Penshurst has been the property of the Sidney family since 1554, and was restored by the architect George Devey in the 1830s.

THE ERA OF LANCASTER AND YORK (1399-1485)

HERSTMONCEUX CASTLE

Hailsham, East Sussex BN27 1RN   Tel: 01323 834444

A remarkable brick castle of the 1440s typical of the ambitious great house projects of the court of Henry VI. It was built by the royal Treasurer Sir Roger Fiennes, who received a licence to erect 'towers and battlements' in 1441. The handsome many-sided towers frame the gatehouse in a powerful and symmetrical entrance elevation.

GREAT CHALFIELD MANOR (NT)

Nr Melksham, Wiltshire SN12 8NH   Tel: 01225 782239

Built in the 1480s by Thomas Tropnell, Great Chalfield is one of the best preserved medieval manor houses in the country, with the hall standing between two cross wings. The gabled porch marks the entrance, and the hall lies to the left. After a long period as a tenant farmhouse, Great Chalfield was carefully restored between 1905 and 1912.

EARLY TUDOR (1485-1547)

HAMPTON COURT PALACE (HRP)

East Molesey, Surrey KT8 9AU   Tel: 08707 527777

The royal palace of Henry VIII, Hampton Court was begun in 1515 as a residence for the king's powerful Chancellor, Cardinal Thomas Wolsey, Archbishop of York; but in 1528 Wolsey's magnificent red-brick palace was forfeit to the crown. Additional work was done for Henry VIII in 1532–5. The palace consisted of three main courts.

HENGRAVE HALL

Bury St Edmunds, Suffolk IP28 6LZ   Tel: 01284 701561

Built between 1525 and 1538 for the wealthy London merchant Thomas Kytson, Hengrave Hall was constructed around a courtyard (with a great hall and three residential ranges), and built out of grey brick and stone from a suppressed monastic house. The window over the entrance is richly decorated with heraldry.

ELIZABETHAN (1558-1603)

BARRINGTON COURT (NT)

Barrington, nr Ilminster, Somerset TA19 0NQ   Tel: 01460 241938

An example of a late 1550s manor house, built by the London merchant William Clifton. The main south front, with its steep gables and pinnacles, is broadly symmetrical, which makes Barrington Court a fine (and early) example of the E-shaped plan, with balanced wings and a central porch.

BURGHLEY HOUSE

Stamford, Lincolnshire PE9 3JY   Tel: 01780 752451

A magnificent stately palace with a distinctive roofline of chimneys cast as Classical columns, Burghley House was built between 1556 and 1587 for William Cecil, Lord Burghley, Lord Treasurer to Queen Elizabeth I. It was built around a large courtyard, with a traditional great hall, dating back to 1556, and an elegant frontispiece of the 1580s.

JACOBEAN (1603-25)

HATFIELD HOUSE

Hatfield, Hertfordshire AL9 5NQ   Tel: 01707 287010

A courtier's house built between 1607 and 1611 by Robert Cecil, 1st Earl of Salisbury, James I's First Minister. This great house was large enough to house the court, its wings being three rooms thick (three-pile), and combines traditional English forms with an elegant Italian-style loggia around the original entrance.

CHASTLETON HOUSE (NT)

Chastleton, nr Moreton-in-Marsh, Glos GL56 0SU   Tel: 01608 674355

A manor house of the early seventeenth century, completed c. 1614 for Walter Jones, a wealthy wool merchant. Although the house was designed with a great hall, the exterior arrangement is notable for its symmetry, effected in the stair towers and gables, and its air of comfortable dignity. The windows are leaded lights within stone mullions and transoms.

CAROLINE (1625-49)

BROOME PARK

Barham, nr Canterbury, Kent CT4 6QX   Tel: 01227 830728

Built in red brick between 1635 and 1638 for Sir Walter Dixwell, this distinctive house conveys a strong sense of symmetry and an ornate roofline, marked by the use of shaped, pedimented gables and dormers, and tall chimneys, with an emphatic use of giant order pilasters. The house forms an H-plan with the central range two rooms deep (double-pile).

WILTON HOUSE

Wilton, Salisbury, Wiltshire SP2 0BJ.   Tel: 01722 746720/01722 746729

The south front of Wilton was built in 1636 for the 4th Earl of Pembroke by the French landscape gardener Isaac de Caus (also known as Isaac de Caux), possibly with advice from Inigo Jones. Wilton draws on Italian sources, notably in the proportions, the pedimented corner towers and the Venetian window at the centre.

RESTORATION/LATER STUART (1660-1702)

SQUERREYS COURT

Westerham, Kent TN16 1SJ   Tel: 01959 562 345 or 563 118

A typical gentry house built around 1680 by Sir Nicholas Crisp in the Classical tradition of Inigo Jones, with a crisply symmetrical elevation of two principal storeys and an attic. A triangular Classical pediment brings emphasis to the centre, and smaller Classical pediments mark the dormer windows.

BELTON HOUSE (NT)

Belton, Grantham, Lincolnshire NG32 2LS   Tel: 01476 566116

Built in *c.* 1684 for the Brownlow family, Belton was modelled on Clarendon House and Coleshill, with an H-shaped plan and a substantial central block (the design now attributed to William Winde). The central cupola and Classical pediment, containing the family arms, are typical of larger Restoration country houses.

QUEEN ANNE (1702-14)

NETHER LYPIATT MANOR (NOP)

Nr Stroud, Gloucestershire

Built for Mr Justice Cox in 1705, the handsome but compact manor has two storeys over a basement, with low symmetrical wings and sash windows of equal heights to both storeys. The symmetry of this delightful and dignified stone-built box is also emphasized by gate-piers on axis to the entrance.

BLENHEIM PALACE

Woodstock, Oxfordshire OX20 1PX   Tel: 08700 602080

Begun in 1705 to designs by John Vanbrugh, and built as a gift to the victorious general the 1st Duke of Marlborough, Blenheim is one of the great palaces of the Queen Anne period, massive and monumental, with great Classical elements given a Baroque twist. Vanbrugh seems to have wanted to evoke the grand mansions of the Elizabethan era, such as Wollaton.

EARLY GEORGIAN (1714-60)

KELMARSH HALL

Kelmarsh, Northampton NN6 9LT   Tel: 01604 686543

Designed by James Gibbs and built by Francis Smith of Warwick in 1728–32 for William Hanbury, Kelmarsh comprises a central Classical block, connected to substantial pavilions by curved wings, which originally contained stables and kitchens.

MEREWORTH CASTLE (NOP)

Mereworth, Kent

A perfect example of the Palladian revival of the reign of George I, designed by Colen Campbell in 1722–25, it is modelled on Palladio's Villa Rotunda, outside Vicenza (also the inspiration for Lord Burlington's Chiswick Villa), with a central domed hall and Classical porticoes on each elevation.

LATER GEORGIAN (1760-1811)

BURTON CONSTABLE HALL

Burton Constable, Skirlaugh, Hull, East Yorkshire HU11 4LN
Tel: 01964 562400

A country house, designed in the 1760s for Sir Marmaduke Wyvill by John Carr. Influenced by Palladio's Villa Emo at Fanzuolo, the raised piano nobile (principal storey) is approached by a double flight of steps up to the colonnaded portico.

KEDLESTON HALL (NT)

Derby, Derbyshire DE22 5JH   Tel: 01332 842191

Built for Sir Nathaniel Curzon, 1759–65, to designs by James Paine, Kedleston was finished by Robert Adam, who also created magnificent interiors. Adam's principal front is a direct evocation of a triumphal arch, and his marble hall a great colonnaded space lined with sculpture that looks directly to ancient Rome for inspiration.

REGENCY (1811-20)

BELVOIR CASTLE

Nr Grantham, Rutland NG32 1PD   Tel: 01476 871000/871002

A castle dating from the eleventh century, and seat of the Dukes of Rutland, Belvoir was transformed in 1801 by James Wyatt's castle style (see page 34). After a fire in 1816, Belvoir was rebuilt to designs by James Thoroton, who had assisted Wyatt, creating a sequence of sumptuous and contrasting interiors, typical of the richness of the finest Regency interiors.

BELSAY HALL (EH)

Belsay Village, Ponteland, Newcastle-upon-Tyne, Northumberland
NE20 0DX   Tel: 01661 881636

Belsay Hall was designed in a severe Greek Revival style by landowner Sir Charles Monck for himself; he moved into the house in 1817. Two bold Doric columns frame the entrance, breaking the solidity of the 100 ft-square stone house, modelled on a Greek temple.

VICTORIAN (1830-1901)

OSBORNE HOUSE (EH)

York Avenue, East Cowes, Isle of Wight PO32 6JY   Tel: 01983 200022

A seaside retreat built for Queen Victoria and designed in the Italianate style by Thomas Cubitt and Prince Albert, with two main ranges (and two distinctive towers), one for family accommodation, the other for reception and guests. Much imitated in the 1840s–70s, Osborne is now a museum, presented in its Victorian character by English Heritage.

CRAGSIDE HOUSE (NT)

Rothbury, Morpeth, Northumberland NE65 7PX   Tel: 01669 620333

A Victorian country house on an elevated site, designed for the 1st Lord Armstrong by Richard Norman Shaw, Cragside was built in the 1870s and 1880s in a version of Old English style, with gables and half-timbering and a varied roofline. It was the first country house to be fully fitted with electricity driven by water power.

EDWARDIAN (1901-10)

MOUNDSMERE MANOR (NOP)

Preston Candover, Basingstoke, Hampshire RG25 2HE

A large country house designed in the 1900s for William Buckley by Reginald Blomfield in the style of Christopher Wren at Hampton Court Palace. Built in red brick with stone dressings, it was completed in 1909. Wren was at this time admired, as (in Blomfield's words) 'the greatest but most English' of all English architects.

GREAT DIXTER

Northiam, Rye, East Sussex TN31 6PH   Tel: 01797 252878

A small, fifteenth-century, half-timbered hall house restored by Nathaniel Lloyd in 1910 and extended for him by Edwin Lutyens, with the addition of a reconstructed timber range, adding a handsome great hall. Famous for its gardens from this period, Great Dixter is still maintained by Lloyd's son, the garden writer Christopher Lloyd.

RIGHT: *A fully blown villa on the Italian model, the Queen's House, Greenwich, was built in 1616 (completed in the 1630s) to designs by Inigo Jones. The first Palladian house in England, the Queen's House marks the beginning of Classically proportioned domestic architecture.*

200 COUNTRY HOUSES TO VISIT

THE FOLLOWING IS A selection of 200 country houses open to the public, which I would recommend, based either on personal experience or some other knowledge of their importance or quality. There are, of course, other houses to be discovered by you. A word of caution: opening times vary considerably, although most houses are open between Easter and October, but some are open more often, others less so. Picking the right time to go is all-important, too. A phone call or visit to a website is essential when arranging a trip. For more detailed information, consult Hudson, Norman, *Hudson's Historic Houses & Gardens: The Comprehensive Annual Guide to Heritage Properties in Great Britain and Ireland* (N. Hudson), or the most recent *National Trust Handbook for Members and Visitors* (The National Trust), or the *English Heritage Members and Visitors Handbook* (English Heritage), all published annually.

ALNWICK CASTLE
Alnwick, Northumberland NE66 1NQ
Tel: 01665 510777
Seat of the Dukes of
Northumberland, of various dates
from the twelfth century, castle
restored by Anthony Salvin in the
nineteenth century.

ALTHORP
Althorp Park, Northampton NN7 4HQ
Tel: 01604 770107
Seat of the Earls Spencer, a late
sixteenth-century house remodelled by
Henry Holland in the late eighteenth
century.

ANGLESEY ABBEY (NT)
Quy Road, Lode, Cambridge,
Cambridgeshire CB5 9EJ
Tel: 01223 810080
The house, modelled from monastic
remains, was restored by the 1st Lord
Fairhaven in the 1920s.

ANTONY HOUSE (NT)
Torpoint, Plymouth, Cornwall PL11 2QA
Tel: 01752 812191
A handsome, early eighteenth-century,
silvery grey-stone country house with
grounds landscaped by Humphry
Repton.

ARBURY HALL
Nuneaton, Warwickshire CV10 7PT
Tel: 02476 382804
An Elizabethan house remodelled in
the mid-eighteenth-century Gothic
Revival style by Henry Keene.

ARLEY HALL AND GARDENS
Northwich, Cheshire CW9 6NA
Tel: 01565 777353
Old manor house substantially rebuilt
in the Elizabethan style in the mid-
nineteenth century.

ARLINGTON COURT (NT)
Arlington, nr Barnstaple, Devon EX31 4LP
Tel: 01271 850296
Neo-classical Regency country house,
designed in 1822 by Thomas Lee for
Colonel John Chichester, whose family
had owned the estate since 1384.

ARUNDEL CASTLE
Arundel, West Sussex BN18 9AB
Tel: 01903 882173

Seat of the Dukes of Norfolk since
1580, the ancient castle, dating from
the 1070s, was restored in an early
English style by the architect C. A.
Buckler in the late nineteenth century.

ASHDOWN HOUSE (NT)
Lambourn, Newbury, Berkshire
RG17 8RE
Tel: 01793 762209
Fine Classical mid-seventeenth-
century house with symmetrical wings.

ASTLEY HALL
Astley Park, Chorley, Lancashire PR7 1NP
Tel: 01257 515555
Timber-framed Tudor house with
seventeenth-century additions.

ATHELHAMPTON HOUSE
Athelhampton, Dorchester, Dorset
DT2 7LG
Tel: 01305 848363
Fifteenth- and sixteenth-century manor
house, partly restored in the late
nineteenth century when the gardens
were also laid out.

ATTINGHAM PARK (NT)
Atcham, Shrewsbury, Shropshire SY4 4TP
Tel: 01743 708162
Late eighteenth-century country
house, designed by George Stewart for
the 1st Lord Berwick, with a picture
gallery by John Nash.

AUCKLAND CASTLE
Bishop Auckland, County Durham
DL14 7NR
Tel: 01388 601627
Historic palace of the Bishop of
Durham, dating from the twelfth,
seventeenth and eighteenth centuries.

AUDLEY END HOUSE (EH)
Saffron Walden, Essex CB11 4JG
Tel: 01799 522842/01799 522399
Major early seventeenth-century
house, with later alterations
(including Robert Adam interiors).

AVEBURY MANOR (NT)
Avebury, nr Marlborough, Wiltshire
SN8 1RF
Tel: 01672 539250
Early sixteenth-century house,
modelled from monastic remains,
restored in the early twentieth century.

BADDESLEY CLINTON (NT)
Rising Lane, Baddesley Clinton Village,
Knowle, Solihull, Warwickshire B93 0DQ
Tel: 01564 783294
A medieval, moated manor house,
mostly dating from the fifteenth century.

BAMBURGH CASTLE
Bamburgh, Northumberland NE69 7DF
Tel: 01668 214515
The castle, dating back to the twelfth
century, was restored, with the
interiors remodelled in the 1890s for
the 1st Lord Armstrong.

BARRINGTON COURT (NT)
Barrington, nr Ilminster, Somerset
TA19 0NQ
Tel: 01460 241938
A sixteenth-century manor house,
the first house to be acquired by the
National Trust; its gardens were laid
out in the 1920s.

BASILDON PARK (NT)
Lower Basildon, Reading, Berkshire
RG8 9NR
Tel: 0118 984 3040
Classical house designed by John Carr
of York in 1776–83, with fine
plasterwork interiors.

BEAULIEU, PALACE HOUSE
Beaulieu, Brockenhurst, Hampshire
SO42 7ZN
Tel: 01590 612345
A thirteenth-century monastic gatehouse,
remodelled for Lord Montagu in the
nineteenth century by Arthur Blomfield.

BELSAY HALL AND GARDENS (EH)
Belsay Village, Ponteland, Newcastle-
upon-Tyne, Northumberland NE20 0DX
Tel: 01661 881636
An early nineteenth-century Greek
Revival mansion, built in 1807–15 for
Sir Charles Monck.

BELTON HOUSE (NT)
Belton, Grantham, Lincolnshire
NG32 2LS
Tel: 01476 566116
A fine country house of 1685–88, with
well-preserved interiors.

BELVOIR CASTLE
Nr Grantham, Rutland NG32 1PD
Tel: 01476 871000/871002

Seat of the Dukes of Rutland, dating from the eleventh century, Belvoir was rebuilt in the early nineteenth century, with a fine series of Regency interiors.

BENINGBROUGH HALL (NT)
Beningbrough, York, North Yorkshire YO30 1DD
Tel: 01904 470666
An early Georgian mansion on the edge of York.

BERKELEY CASTLE
Gloucestershire GL13 9BQ
Tel: 01453 810332
Seat of the Berkeley family since the twelfth century, the castle was rebuilt in the fourteenth century, then restored in the 1920s.

BERRINGTON HALL (NT)
Nr Leominster, Herefordshire HR6 0DW
Tel: 01568 615721
Elegant, late eighteenth-century Georgian house, designed by Henry Holland, is set in parkland landscaped by Lancelot Brown.

BLACKWELL
Bowness-on-Windermere, Cumbria LA22 3JR
Tel: 01539 446139
Early twentieth-century house overlooking Windermere, designed by the Arts and Crafts architect M. H. Baillie Scott.

BLENHEIM PALACE
Woodstock, Oxfordshire OX20 1PX
Tel: 08700 602080
English Baroque palace designed by John Vanbrugh for the 1st Duke of Marlborough.

BLICKLING HALL (NT)
Blickling, Norwich, Norfolk NR11 6NF
Tel: 01263 738030
Early seventeenth-century manor house, with important seventeenth- and eighteenth-century interiors.

BODIAM CASTLE (NT)
Bodiam, nr Robertsbridge, East Sussex TN32 5UA
Tel: 01580 830436
Ruins of a fine moated castle, built in 1385, with the exterior mostly intact.

BOLSOVER CASTLE, the 'LITTLE CASTLE BOLSOVER' (EH)
Castle Street, Bolsover, Derbyshire S44 6PR
Tel: 01246 822844
Originally a twelfth-century castle, Bolsover was rebuilt in c. 1621 by John Smythson for Sir Charles Cavendish, with the addition of a new hall and state rooms during the late seventeenth century.

BOUGHTON HOUSE
Boughton, Kettering, Northamptonshire NN16 9UP
Tel: 01536 515731
Built in the late seventeenth century in the French style, for the 1st Duke of Montagu (now a seat of the Dukes of Buccleuch and Queensberry).

BRAMHAM PARK
Wetherby, West Yorkshire LS23 6ND
Tel: 01937 846000
Early eighteenth-century country house with the best preserved French-inspired formal gardens in England.

BRODSWORTH HALL (EH)
Brodsworth, nr Doncaster, Yorkshire DN5 7XJ
Tel: 01302 722598
Victorian country house designed in the Italianate style, and preserved 'as found' in its later twentieth-century decline.

BROUGHTON CASTLE
Broughton, Banbury, Oxfordshire OX15 5EB
Tel: 01295 722547
Original moated manor house of c. 1300, rebuilt in the mid-sixteenth century.

BROWSHOLME HALL
Clitheroe Road, Cowark, Clitheroe, Lancashire BB7 3DE
Tel: 01254 827160/01254 826719
An early sixteenth-century house, with interiors altered by James Wyatt during the eighteenth century.

BURGHLEY HOUSE
Stamford, Lincolnshire PE9 3JY
Tel: 01780 752451
An Elizabethan great house with the main interiors remodelled by William Talman in the late seventeenth century.

BURTON AGNES HALL
Burton Agnes, Driffield, Yorkshire YO25 0ND
Tel: 01262 490324
Early seventeenth-century country house, designed by Robert Smythson, with a magnificent carved hall screen.

CADHAY
Ottery St. Mary, Devon EX11 1QT
Tel: 01404 812432/01404 812962
Sixteenth-century manor house (incorporating 1470s work) restored in the early twentieth century.

CAERHAYS CASTLE
Caerhays, Gorran, St Austell, Cornwall PL26 6LY
Tel: 01872 501310
Early nineteenth-century Picturesque castle designed by John Nash.

CALKE ABBEY (NT)
Ticknall, Derby, Derbyshire DE73 1LE
Tel: 01332 863822
Originally an Elizabethan house, built on the site of a twelfth-century priory, Calke Abbey was remodelled in 1702–04 for Sir John Harpur. The interior is now preserved 'as found' to illustrate twentieth-century decline.

CANONS ASHBY HOUSE (NT)
Canons Ashby, Daventry, Northamptonshire NN11 3SD
Tel: 01327 861900
Elizabethan manor house, with some early eighteenth-century alterations.

CASTLE DROGO (NT)
Drewsteignton, nr Exeter EX6 6PB
Tel: 01647 433306
An early twentieth-century granite-built castle overlooking Dartmoor, designed for the millionaire Julius Drewe by Sir Edwin Lutyens, with sumptuous, medieval-style interiors.

CASTLE HOWARD
York, North Yorkshire YO60 7DA
Tel: 01653 648444
Stupendous 1690s country house designed by John Vanbrugh for the Earl of Carlisle.

CHARLECOTE PARK (NT)
Warwick, Warwickshire CV35 9ER
Tel: 01789 470277
Sixteenth-century manor house,
restored in the nineteenth century.

CHASTLETON HOUSE (NT)
Chastleton, nr Moreton-in-Marsh,
Gloucestershire GL56 0SU
Tel: 01608 674355
Early seventeenth-century manor
house, built in Cotswold stone, with a
Renaissance astronomical garden and
ring of topiary.

CHATSWORTH
Bakewell, Derbyshire DE45 1PP
Tel: 01246 565300
The seat of the Dukes of Devonshire,
a sixteenth-century house remodelled
in the late seventeenth and
nineteenth centuries.

CHAVENAGE HOUSE
Tetbury, Gloucestershire GL8 8XP
Tel: 01666 502329
A Cotswold-stone Elizabethan manor
house, with minor alterations in the
early nineteenth and early twentieth
centuries.

CHETTLE HOUSE
Chettle, Blandford Forum, Dorset
DT11 8DB
Tel: 01258 830858
A fine example of an English Baroque
manor house, designed by Thomas
Archer in 1710, with later renovations
in 1846 and 1912.

CHICHELEY HALL
Chicheley, Newport Pagnell,
Buckinghamshire MK16 9JJ
Tel: 01234 391 252
A fine early Georgian country house,
designed for Sir John Chester in
1719–23 by Francis Smith of Warwick,
with decoration by William Kent.

CHIDDINGSTONE CASTLE
Nr Edenbridge, Kent TN8 7AD
Tel: 01892 870347
Tudor house remodelled by William
Atkinson in Georgian Gothic style in
the early nineteenth century.

CHILLINGHAM CASTLE
Chillingham, Alnwick,
Northumberland NE66 5NJ
Tel: 01668 215359
Fourteenth-century castle, with
sixteenth-century additions and some
later remodelling.

CLANDON PARK (NT)
West Clandon, Guildford, Surrey
GU4 7RQ
Tel: 01483 222482
Palladian country house designed in
the 1730s by the Venetian architect
Giacomo Leoni for the 2nd Lord
Onslow, with a two-storeyed Marble
Hall and chimneypieces by the
sculptor John Rysbrack.

CLAYDON HOUSE (NT)
Middle Claydon, nr Buckingham,
Buckinghamshire MK18 2EY
Tel: 01296 730349
Eighteenth-century house with
unusual Rococo and chinoiserie
decoration. Originally a Jacobean
manor house, Claydon was remodelled
in the 1760s by the 2nd Lord Verney.

COBHAM HALL
Cobham Hall, Cobham, Kent
DA12 3BL
Tel: 01474 823371
Sixteenth-century house, remodelled
in the seventeenth century and then
again by James Wyatt in the late
eighteenth and early nineteenth
centuries, with parkland landscaped by
Humphry Repton. Cobham Hall is
now an independent school for girls.

CORSHAM COURT
Corsham, Wiltshire SN13 0BZ
Tel: 01249 701610
Elizabethan house with alterations
made to the park and house by
Lancelot 'Capability' Brown.

COTEHELE (NT)
St Dominick, nr Saltash, Cornwall
PL12 6TA
Tel: 01579 351346
Little-altered medieval moated
manor house, built in granite and
slatestone for the Edgecumbe family
between 1485 and 1627, with a
collection of original furniture,
armour and tapestries.

COTHAY MANOR
Greenham, Wellington, Somerset
TA21 0JR
Tel: 01823 672283
An important fourteenth-century
manor house, with some early
seventeenth-century and early
twentieth-century additions.

COTTESBROOKE HALL
Cottesbrooke, Northamptonshire
NN6 8PF
Tel: 01604 505808
Early eighteenth-century country
house, the central block with flanking
pavilions, attributed to Francis Smith
of Warwick.

CRAGSIDE HOUSE (NT)
Rothbury, Morpeth, Northumberland
NE65 7PX
Tel: 01669 620333/620150
Late nineteenth-century country
house in Old English styles designed
by Richard Norman Shaw for the 1st
Lord Armstrong.

DALEMAIN
Penrith, Cumbria CA11 0HB
Tel: 01768 486450
Late seventeenth-century country
house, refronted in the eighteenth
century.

DANSON HOUSE
Danson Park, Danson Road,
Bexleyheath, Kent DA6 7AA
Tel: 0208 303 6699
A villa designed in the 1760s by Sir
Robert Taylor for the London
merchant Sir John Boyd, with
additions by Sir William Chambers.

DEENE PARK
Corby, Northamptonshire
NN17 3EW
Tel: 01780 450278
Sixteenth-century country house,
extended in the later eighteenth
century.

DITCHLEY PARK
Enstone, Oxfordshire OX7 4ER
Tel: 01608 677346
Eighteenth-century house designed by
James Gibbs, with interiors by
William Kent and Henry Flitcroft.

DODDINGTON HALL
Nr Nether Stowey, Bridgwater,
Somerset TA5 1LF
Tel: 01278 741400
Sixteenth-century manor house in
semi-formal garden.

DOWN HOUSE
Downe, Kent BR6 7JT
Tel: 01689 859119
The early nineteenth-century country
home of Charles Darwin.

DUNCOMBE PARK
Helmsley, North Yorkshire YO62 5EB
Tel: 01439 770213
Early eighteenth-century country
house designed by William
Wakefield, with landscaped gardens.

DUNHAM MASSEY (NT)
Altrincham, Cheshire WA14 4SJ
Tel: 0161 941 1025
Early Georgian house with important
Edwardian interiors.

DYRHAM PARK (NT)
Dyrham, nr Chippenham,
Gloucestershire SN14 8ER
Tel: 0117 9372501
A Baroque country house, built
c. 1691–1702 and designed by
William Talman for William
Blathwayt, Secretary at War during
the reign of William III.

EASTNOR CASTLE
Nr Ledbury, Herefordshire HR8 1RL
Tel: 01531 633160
Early nineteenth-century castle
designed by Robert Smirke in the
manner of a medieval Welsh-border
fortress.

ELTON HALL
Elton, nr Peterborough PE8 6SH
Tel: 01832 280468
Of fifteenth-century origins, Elton was
much remodelled in the Gothic
Revival style during the late eighteenth
and early nineteenth centuries.

ERDDIG HALL (NT)
Wrexham, North Wales LL13 0YT
Tel: 01978 355314

Designed by Thomas Webb in 1687,
the originally square house was extended
in the 1720s, when wings were added;
and in the 1770s the west front was faced
in stone.

EUSTON HALL
Euston, Thetford, Norfolk IP24 2QP
Tel: 01842 766366
Seat of the Dukes of Grafton, with the
surviving range of the late seventeenth-
century house. The landscaped park
was designed by William Kent.

FARNBOROUGH HALL (NT)
Farnborough, Banbury, Warwickshire
OX17 1DU
Tel: 01295 690002
Mid-eighteenth-century, stone-built
house with fine plasterwork
decoration and landscaped garden.

FELBRIGG HALL (NT)
Felbrigg, Norwich, Norfolk NR11 8PR
Tel: 01263 837444
Country house of early and late
seventeenth-century building periods,
with important Grand Tour
collections.

FIRLE PLACE
Firle, Lewes, East Sussex BN8 6LP
Tel: 01273 858567
Tudor house remodelled in the style
of a French chateau.

FORDE ABBEY
Chard, Somerset TA20 4LU
Tel: 01460 220231
Monastic remains remodelled in the
seventeenth century.

FOUNTAINS HALL (NT)
Fountains, Studley Royal, Ripon,
North Yorkshire HG4 3DY
Tel: 01765 608888
A sixteenth-century mansion built
partly with stone from the ruins of the
nearby Fountains Abbey, the hall house
reflects the style of the Elizabethan
architect Robert Smythson.

FRAMPTON COURT
Frampton-on-Severn, Gloucestershire
GL2 7EU
Tel: 01452 740267
Built in 1731–33 in the manner of
John Vanbrugh, and attributed to
James Strahan.

GLYNDE PLACE
Glynde, Nr Lewes, East Sussex BN8 6SX
Tel: 01273 858224
Sixteenth-century flint and brick
house, with seventeenth- and
eighteenth-century alterations.

GODOLPHIN COURT (NT)
Godolphin Court, Godolphin Cross,
Helston, TR13 9RE
Tel: 01736 762479
Seventeenth-century house with
fifteenth-century towers.

GOODWOOD HOUSE
Goodwood, Chichester, West Sussex
PO18 0PX
Tel: 01243 755040
Seat of the Dukes of Richmond
substantially rebuilt in the late
eighteenth century by James Wyatt.

GREAT CHALFIELD MANOR (NT)
Nr Melksham, Wiltshire SN12 8NH
Tel: 01225 782239
Dating from 1480, the manor and
gardens were restored at the
beginning of the last century.

GREAT DIXTER
Northiam, Rye, East Sussex TN31 6PH
Tel: 01797 252878
The fifteenth-century hall house was
restored and extended in 1910 by
Edwin Lutyens.

GRIMSTHORPE CASTLE
Grimsthorpe, Bourne, Lincolnshire
PE10 0LY
Tel: 01778 591205
The castle's North Front is Sir John
Vanbrugh's last major work.

HADDON HALL
Bakewell, Derbyshire DE45 1LA
Tel: 01629 812855
A medieval and Tudor manor house
that has survived almost unaltered
since the late sixteenth century, and
was restored in the 1920s.

HAGLEY HALL
Hagley, Worcestershire DY9 9LG
Tel: 01562 882408
The last great Palladian house,
designed by Sanderson Miller in 1753.

Ham House (NT)
Ham Street, Ham, Richmond-upon-Thames, Surrey TW10 7RS
Tel: 020 8940 1950
A seventeenth-century grand house on the banks of the Thames, built in 1610 and extended during the 1670s by the extravagant Duchess of Lauderdale.

Hampton Court Palace (HRP)
East Molesey, Surrey KT8 9AU
Tel: 08707 527777
Henry VIII's magnificent early sixteenth-century riverside palace.

Hanbury Hall (NT)
School Road, Droitwich, Worcestershire WR9 7EA
Tel: 01527 821214
Handsome country house built in 1701, representing the finest Restoration taste, with a fine painted staircase.

Hardwick Hall (NT)
Doe Lea, Chesterfield, Derbyshire S44 5QJ
Tel: 01246 850430
A late sixteenth-century grand prodigy' house, built for Bess of Hardwick.

Harewood House
Harewood, Leeds, West Yorkshire LS17 9LQ
Tel: 0113 2181010
Eighteenth-century house designed by Robert Adam, extended and remodelled by Sir Charles Barry in the nineteenth century.

Harlaxton Manor
Harlaxton, Grantham, Lincolnshire NG32 1AG
Tel: 01476 403000
Early nineteenth-century neo-Elizabethan house with unusual mixture of interior architectural styles.

Hatchlands Park (NT)
East Clandon, Guildford, Surrey GU4 7RT
Tel: 01483 222482
Mid-eighteenth-century house, with fine Robert Adam interiors and wooded park landscaped by Humphry Repton, home to the historic Cobbe Collection of Old Master paintings, portraits and keyboard instruments.

Hatfield House
Hatfield, Hertfordshire AL9 5NQ
Tel: 01707 287010
An early seventeenth-century Jacobean courtier's house, Hatfield House was built in 1611 by Robert Cecil, 1st Earl of Salisbury, with gardens designed by John Tradescent the Elder.

Hengrave Hall
Bury St Edmunds, Suffolk IP28 6LZ
Tel: 01284 701561
Early sixteenth-century manor house, built around a courtyard (originally moated).

Hever Castle
Hever, Edenbridge Kent TN8 7NG
Tel: 01732 865224
Fifteenth-century moated manor house, restored in the early twentieth century for the 1st Lord Astor.

Highclere Castle
Highclere, nr Newbury, Berkshire RG20 9RN
Tel: 01635 253210
Country house remodelled in the early nineteenth century in neo-Elizabethan style by Charles Barry.

Hoghton Tower
Hoghton, Preston, Lancashire PR5 0SH
Tel: 01254 852986
Sixteenth-century house with additions of c. 1700 restored in the nineteenth century.

Holkham Hall
Wells-next-the-Sea, Norfolk, NR23 1AB
Tel: 01328 710227
Eighteenth-century Palladian-style mansion, built to designs by William Kent, Mathew Brettingham and the 1st Earl of Leicester.

Honington Hall
Shipston-on-Stour, Warwickshire CV36 5AA
Tel: 01608 661434
Red-brick house, dating from the 1680s, with the interiors altered in the mid-eighteenth century.

Houghton Hall
Houghton, King's Lynn, Norfolk PE31 6UE
Tel: 01485 528569

Built in the 1720s and 1730s for Sir Robert Walpole to designs by James Gibbs.

Hutton-in-the-Forest
Skelton, Penrith, Cumbria CA11 9TH
Tel: 017684 84449
Originally a medieval stronghold with a surviving pele tower, Hutton has been much altered and extended from the seventeenth to nineteenth centuries.

Ickworth House (NT)
The Rotunda, Horringer, Bury St Edmunds, Suffolk IP29 5QE
Tel: 01284 735270
Late eighteenth-century house with a huge rotunda, completed in the 1820s.

Ightham Mote (NT)
Ivy Hatch, Sevenoaks, Kent TN15 0NT
Tel: 01732 810378
Moated manor house dating from 1330, with later alterations.

Kedleston Hall (NT)
Derby, Derbyshire DE22 5JH
Tel: 01332 842191
Palladian mansion built in 1759–65 for the Curzon family, with interiors and parkland designed by Robert Adam.

Kelmarsh Hall
Kelmarsh, Northampton NN6 9LT
Tel: 01604 686543
Early eighteenth-century house designed by James Gibbs.

Kelmscott Manor
Kelmscott, Lechlade, Oxfordshire GL7 3HJ
Tel: 01367 252486
Sixteenth-century manor house, leased by William Morris as his summer home in the late nineteenth century.

Kentwell Hall
Long Melford, Suffolk CO10 9BA
Tel: 01787 310207
Moated Tudor manor house, with some of the interiors altered in the 1820s in the Gothic style of Thomas Hopper.

Kingston Bagpuize House
Kingston Bagpuize, nr Abingdon,

Late seventeenth-century red-brick house, with handsome panelled interiors.

KINGSTON LACY (NT)
Wimborne Minster, Dorset BH21 4EA
Tel: 01202 883402
Seventeenth-century house, remodelled in the early nineteenth century by Charles Barry.

KIRBY HALL (EH)
Gretton, nr Corby, Northamptonshire
NN17 5EN
Tel: 01536 203230
Richly decorated Elizabethan mansion built for the courtier Sir Christopher Hatton.

KNEBWORTH HOUSE
Knebworth, Hertfordshire SG3 6PY
Tel: SG3 6PY 01438 812661
Remnant of a sixteenth-century country house, remodelled as a Romantic Gothic Revival house in the early eighteenth century.

KNOLE (NT)
Sevenoaks, Kent TN15 0RP
Tel: 01732 462100
Mid-sixteenth-century house remodelled in the early seventeenth century.

LACOCK ABBEY (NT)
Lacock, nr Chippenham, Wiltshire
SN15 2LG
Tel: 01249 730459
The medieval abbey, founded in 1232, was converted into a country house c. 1540, retaining the original cloisters, sacristy, chapter house and monastic rooms.

LAMPORT HALL
Lamport, Northampton, NN6 9HD
Tel: 01604 686272
Mid-seventeenth-century house, designed by John Webb, with wings added in the eighteenth century.

LANHYDROCK (NT)
Bodmin, Cornwall PL30 5AD
Tel: 01208 265950
Seventeenth-century house, rebuilt after a fire in 1881 for the 1st Lord Robartes.

LAYER MARNEY TOWER
Nr Colchester, Essex CO5 9US
Tel: 01206 330784
A fine Tudor gatehouse, dating from 1520, built by Henry the 1st Lord Marney, Lord Privy Seal to Henry VIII.

LEEDS CASTLE
Leeds, Nr Maidstone, Kent ME17 1PL
Tel: 01622 765400
Thirteenth- and fourteenth-century moated castle, with interiors remodelled by Lady Baillie in the 1920s.

LEVENS HALL
Kendal, Cumbria LA8 0PD
Tel: 01539 560321
An Elizabethan house incorporating an earlier pele tower.

LINDISFARNE CASTLE (NT)
Holy Island, Berwick-upon-Tweed,
Northumberland TD15 2SH
Tel: 01289 389244
Built in 1550, and converted in 1903 into a private house for Edward Hudson by Edwin Lutyens.

LITTLE MORETON HALL (NT)
Congleton, Cheshire CW12 4SD
Tel: 01260 272018
A fine timber-framed moated manor of two sixteenth-century building dates.

LONGLEAT
Warminster, Wiltshire BA12 7NW
Tel: 01985 844400
Seat of the Marquises of Bath, Longleat is an important Elizabethan mansion with nineteenth-century interiors.

LOSELEY PARK
Guildford, Surrey GU23 1HS
Tel: 01483 405120
A house built in 1562–68 from the stone of a demolished abbey.

LULLINGSTONE CASTLE
Lullingstone Park, Eynsford, Dartford,
Kent DA4 0JA
Tel: 07810 355 199
Fifteenth-century brick gatehouse, remodelled in the early eighteenth century.

LULWORTH CASTLE (EH)
East Lulworth, Wareham, Dorset
BH20 5QS

Tel: 01929 400352
Built as a seventeenth-century hunting lodge, the castle was gutted by fire in 1929, but recently re-roofed by English Heritage.

LYDIARD HOUSE
Lydiard Tregoze, Swindon, Wiltshire
SN5 9PA
Tel: 01793 770401
Country house, dating from the 1740s, with important mid-eighteenth-century decoration, now a museum.

LYME PARK (NT)
Disley, Stockport, Cheshire SK12 2NX
Tel: 01663 762023
Elizabethan house with early eighteenth-century Classical additions by Giacomo Leoni.

MADRESFIELD COURT
Madresfield, Malvern WR13 5AU
Tel: 01684 573614
A sixteenth-century moated manor house rebuilt in the nineteenth century by Philip Hardwick.

MANOR, THE
Hemingford Grey, Huntingdon,
Cambridgeshire PE28 9BN
Tel: 01480 463134
A twelfth-century house believed to be one of the oldest houses to have been continuously inhabited in Britain.

MAPLEDURHAM HOUSE
Mapledurham, Reading, Berkshire
RG4 7TR
Tel: 01189 723350
Red-brick, sixteenth-century house (reputed to be the model for Toad Hall in Kenneth Grahame's story *The Wind in the Willows* [1908]).

MAPPERTON
Beaminster, Dorset DT8 3NR
Tel: 01308 862645
A sixteenth-century house, extended in the 1660s, with the interiors remodelled in the eighteenth century.

MARKENFIELD HALL
Nr Ripon, North Yorkshire HG4 3AD
Tel: 01765 603411
An important moated manor house built in 1310.

MELFORD HALL (NT)
Long Melford, Sudbury, Suffolk
CO10 9AA
Tel: 01787 379228
A little-altered Tudor mansion house
with turrets.

MIREHOUSE
Keswick, Cumbria CA12 4QE
Tel: 01786 772287
Seventeenth-century house extended
during the eighteenth and nineteenth
centuries, with links to the Romantic
poets Lord Alfred Tennyson and
William Wordsworth.

MOCCAS COURT
Moccas, Herefordshire HR2 9LH
Tel: 01981 500019
Eighteenth-century house designed by
Anthony Keck, with interiors by
Robert Adam.

MONTACUTE HOUSE (NT)
Montacute, Somerset TA15 6XP
Tel: 01935 823289
One of the finest late sixteenth-
century Elizabethan houses, built for
Sir Edward Phelips, with Renaissance
plasterwork, chimneys and glass and
the longest long gallery in England.

MOTTISFONT ABBEY (NT)
Mottisfont, nr Romsey, Hampshire
SO51 0LP
Tel: 01794 340757
A twelfth-century priory, Mottisfont
Abbey was converted into a house after
the Dissolution. During the 1930s, the
drawing room was decorated by Rex
Whistler, a master of imaginative
trompe-l'oeil.

MUNCASTER CASTLE
Ravenglass, Cumbria CA18 1RQ
Tel: 01229 717614
Fourteenth-century origins, restored
and rebuilt by Anthony Salvin in the
later nineteenth century.

NEWBY HALL
Ripon, North Yorkshire HG4 5AE
Tel: 0845 4504068
Built in the 1690s, designed with
Robert Adam interiors and furnished
with original Chippendale furniture.

NEWSTEAD ABBEY
Newstead Abbey Park, Ravenshead,
Nottinghamshire NG15 8NA
Tel: 01623 455900
Founded as an Augustinian monastery
in the late twelfth century, Newstead
Abbey was converted into a house by
Sir John Byron in the 1540s, and
remodelled in the mid-nineteenth
century. The abbey was home to the
poet Lord Byron, who sold it in 1818.

NORTON CONYERS
Nr Ripon, North Yorkshire HG4 5EQ
Tel: 01765 640333
Sixteenth- and seventeenth-century
country house, with distinctive Dutch
gables.

NOSTELL PRIORY
Doncaster Road, Wakefield,
West Yorkshire WF4 1QE
Tel: 01924 863892
Eighteenth-century house designed by
James Paine, with additional interiors
by Robert Adam and furniture by
Thomas Chippendale.

OLD WARDOUR CASTLE (EH)
Nr Tisbury, Wiltshire SP3 6RR
Tel: 01747 870487
An unusual six-sided castle built in the
late fourteenth century for John, the 5th
Lord Lovel, Wardour was adapted in
the sixteenth century, and surrounded
by a landscaped park in the eighteenth
century, but is now a ruin.

OSBORNE HOUSE (EH)
York Avenue, East Cowes,
Isle of Wight P032 6JY
Tel: 01983 200022
Seaside retreat of Queen Victoria,
designed by Prince Albert and
Thomas Cubitt.

OSTERLEY PARK (NT)
Jersey Road, Isleworth, Middlesex
TW7 4RB
Tel: 020 8232 5050
Sixteenth-century house, transformed
by Robert Adam in the 1760s, with
magnificent interiors.

OWLPEN MANOR
Nr Uley, Gloucestershire GL11 5BZ

Tel: 01453-860261
Tudor manor house, built in
1450–1616, with Cotswold Arts and
Crafts associations.

OXBURGH HALL (NT)
Oxborough, King's Lynn, Norfolk
PE33 9PS
Tel: 01366 328258
Moated manor house built in 1482,
its interiors remodelled in the
nineteenth century.

PACKWOOD HOUSE (NT)
Lapworth, Solihull, Warwickshire
B94 6AT
Tel: 01564 783294
Sixteenth-century manor house
restored in the early twentieth century.

PAINSHILL PARK
Portsmouth Road, Cobham, Surrey
KT11 1JE
Tel: 01932 868113
Important eighteenth-century
landscaped park designed by the Hon.
Charles Hamilton.

PARHAM HOUSE
Parham Park, Storrington, nr
Pulborough, West Sussex RH20 4HS
Tel: 01903 742021
Elizabethan manor house restored in
the 1920s by the Pearson family.

PENSHURST PLACE
Penshurst, Nr Tonbridge, Kent TN11 8DG
Tel: 01892 870307
Medieval house with later improvements, housing a collection from the
fifteenth, sixteenth and seventeenth
centuries.

PETWORTH HOUSE (NT)
Petworth, Sussex GU28 0AE
Tel: 01798 342207
Magnificent late seventeenth-century
house, with carvings by Grinling
Gibbons.

PLAS NEWYDD (NT)
Llanfairpwll, Anglesey, Wales LL61 6DQ
Tel: 01248 714795
An elegant eighteenth-century
mansion, designed by James Wyatt, set
in grounds on the banks of the Menai
Strait with views over Anglesey and
Snowdownia. Seat of the Marquess of
Anglesey, its interiors were restyled in
the 1930s, with mural by Rex Whistler.

POWDERHAM CASTLE
Kenton, Exeter, Devon EX6 8JQ
Tel: 01626 890243
Built in 1390, with eighteenth-century
additions.

PRIDEAUX PLACE
Padstow, Cornwall PL28 8RP
Tel: 01841 532411
Sixteenth-century house remodelled
in Georgian Gothic style in the early
nineteenth century.

QUEEN'S HOUSE
Greenwich, London SE10 9NF
Tel: 0208 858 4422
Early seventeenth-century house
designed by Inigo Jones, completed in
the 1630s.

RABY CASTLE
Staindrop, Darlington, County
Durham DL2 3AH
Tel: 01833 660202/660888
Seat of Lord Barnard, dating from the
Middle Ages, eighteenth and
nineteenth centuries.

RAGLEY HALL
Alcester, Warwickshire B49 5NH
Tel: 01789 762090
Late seventeenth-century house,
completed in the mid-eighteenth
century, partly by James Gibbs.

RENISHAW HALL
Renishaw, Sheffield, Derbyshire
S21 3WB
Tel: 01246 432310
Seventeenth-century house, extended
around 1800, with important
Italianate gardens dating from the
early twentieth century.

ROCKINGHAM CASTLE
Rockingham, Market Harborough,
Leicestershire LE16 8TH
Tel: 01536 770240
Medieval castle with sixteenth- and
seventeenth-century alterations,
restored in the nineteenth century by
Anthony Salvin.

SALTRAM (NT)
Plympton, Plymouth, Devon
PL7 1UH
Tel: 01752 333500
Important eighteenth-century house
with interiors by Robert Adam.

SANDRINGHAM HOUSE
Sandringham, Norfolk PE35 6EN
Tel: 01553 772675
Neo-Jacobean house built in 1870 for
the Prince of Wales (later Edward VII).
Country home of H. M. The Queen.

SCAMPSTON HALL
Malton, North Yorkshire YO17 8NG
Tel: 01944 759111
Handsome house of around 1800
designed by Thomas Leverton.

BELOW: *Ragley Hall,
Warwickshire, designed in the late
17th century, was mostly
completed in the mid-18th century,
with an Ionic portico added by
James Wyatt in the 1780s.*

SEATON DELAVAL HALL (EH)
Seaton Sluice, nr Whitley Bay,
Northumberland NE26 4QR
Tel: 0191 2371493/0786
Powerful design by John Vanbrugh
for Admiral George Delaval,
completed in the 1720s, partially
destroyed by fire in 1822, but restored
later in the nineteenth century.

SHERBORNE CASTLE
Sherborne Castle, Cheap Street,
Sherborne, Dorset DT9 3PY
Tel: 01935 813182
Elizabethan country house extended
in the eighteenth and nineteenth
centuries.

SISSINGHURST CASTLE GARDEN (NT)
Sissinghurst, nr Cranbrook, Kent
TN17 2AB
Tel: 01580 710700
Remnants of an Elizabethan house
that became the setting for the gardens
created by Vita Sackville-West.

SLEDMERE HOUSE
Sledmere Park, Sledmere, Driffield,
East Yorkshire YO25 0XG
Tel: 01377 236637
Mid-eighteenth-century house,
restored after a major fire in 1911.

SNOWSHILL MANOR (NT)
Snowshill, nr Broadway,
Gloucestershire WR12 7JU
Tel: 01386 852410
Handsome Cotswold manor house,
restored in the early twentieth
century, with unusual collections.

SOMERLEYTON HALL
Lowestoft, Suffolk NR32 5QQ
Tel: 08712 224244
Great Victorian country house
designed in neo-Jacobean style by
John Thomas.

SPEKE HALL (NT)
The Walk, Speke, Merseyside,
Liverpool L24 1XD
Tel: 01514 277 231
Half-timbered house dating from
1490, with some fine early
seventeenth-century plasterwork.

SQUERRYES COURT
Westerham, Kent TN16 1SJ
Tel: 01959 562 345 or 563 118
Late seventeenth-century red-brick
manor house built by Sir Nicholas Crisp
on the site of a twelfth-century manor
belonging to the de Squerie family.

STANDEN (NT)
West Hoathly Road, East Grinstead,
Sussex RH19 4NE
Tel: 01342 323029
House designed in the 1890s by Philip
Webb and furnished by Morris and Co.

STANFORD HALL
Lutterworth, Leicestershire LE17 6DH
Tel: 01788 860250
Late seventeenth-century William and
Mary house on the banks of the River
Avon, designed by William Smith of
Warwick, with fine 1690s interiors.

STANSTED PARK
Rowlands Castle, Hampshire PO9 6DX
Tel: 02392 412265
Eighteenth-century house designed by
James Wyatt, and restored by Arthur
Blomfield after a fire in 1900.

STANWAY HOUSE
Stanway, Cheltenham,
Gloucestershire GL54 5PQ
Tel: 01386 584469 /01386 584528
Romantic seventeenth-century Jacobean
manor house, with monastic origins and
a nineteenth-century water garden.

STONOR
Stonor Park, Henley-on-Thames,
Oxfordshire RG9 6HF
Tel: 01491 638587
A Tudor manor house, set within a
deer park and built around a twelfth-
century dwelling, Stonor was sub-
sequently remodelled in the sixteenth
century, with the addition of sash
windows in the eighteenth century.

STOURHEAD (NT)
Stourton, Warminster, Wiltshire
BA12 6QD
Tel: 01747 841152
A Palladian house of the 1720s, with
an exceptional landscape garden of
the 1740s–80s.

STOWE LANDSCAPE GARDENS (NT)
Buckingham, Buckinghamshire
MK18 5EH
Tel: 01494 755568/01280 822850
The finest eighteenth-century
landscape gardens with Arcadian
temples and statues.

STRATFIELD SAYE HOUSE
Stratfield Saye, Reading, Berkshire
RG7 2BZ
Tel: 01256 882882
Originally a Jacobean house, built by
Sir William Pitt in 1630, Stratfield
was acquired by the 1st Duke of
Wellington in 1817 with a gift of
money from a grateful nation. The
Duke added the conservatory in 1838
and the outer wings in 1846.

TATTON PARK (NT)
Knutsford, Cheshire WA16 6QN
Tel: 01625 534400
Early nineteenth-century Classical
house designed by Samuel Wyatt,
retaining a Tudor hall.

TEMPLE NEWSAM
Leeds, West Yorkshire LS15 0AD
Tel: 01132 647321
Important sixteenth- and seventeenth-
century house with eighteenth-
century interiors, now a museum with
an important furniture collection.

TISSINGTON HALL
Tissington, Ashbourne, Derbyshire
DE6 1RA
Tel: 01335 352200
Sixteenth-century manor house,
with gates by Robert Bakewell. The
west front was refaced in a Classical
style in the eighteenth century.

TREDEGAR HOUSE
Newport, Gwent, South Wales
NP10 HYW
Tel: 01633 815880
A fine, barely altered later seventeenth-
century house, now a museum.

TRERICE (NT)
Kestle Mill, nr Newquay, Cornwall
TR8 4PG
Tel: 01637 875404

A small, secluded Elizabethan manor house built in 1573 by Sir John Arundel, with unusual Dutch-style scroll gables, and the original Elizabethan plasterwork and glass.

TYNTESFIELD (NT)
Wraxall, Bristol, North Somerset BS48 1NT
Tel: 08704 584500
Victorian country house, with a chapel designed by Arthur Blomfield.

UGBROOKE HOUSE AND PARK
Chudleigh, Newton Abbot, Devon TQ13 0AD
Tel: 01626 852179
Originally a Tudor manor, built around an eleventh-century house, Ugbrooke was remodelled in the 1760s in Robert Adam's castle style; and the grounds were landscaped by Capability Brown.

UPPARK (NT)
South Harting, Petersfield, Sussex GU31 5QR
Tel: 01730 825415
Imposing late seventeenth-century house on the South Downs, recently restored after a major fire.

VYNE, THE (NT)
Sherborne St John, Basingstoke, Hampshire RG24 9HL
Tel: 01256 883858
Sixteenth-century house, with mid-seventeenth-century Classical portico and eighteenth-century alterations.

WADDESDON MANOR (NT)
Waddesdon, nr Aylesbury, Buckinghamshire HP18 0JH
Tel: 01296 653203/01296 653211
Built 1874–89 for Baron Ferdinand de Rothschild in the style of a sixteenth-century French chateau.

WALLINGTON (NT)
Cambo, Morpeth, Northumberland NE61 4AR
Tel: 01670 773600
Later seventeenth-century house, with fine Rococo interiors and nineteenth-century wall-paintings.

WARWICK CASTLE
Warwick, Warwickshire CV34 4QU
Tel: 0870 442 2000

Built as a medieval fortress in 1068, as part of a defensive chain created by William I, the Norman castle was later reconstructed, extended and embellished in the fourteenth, seventeenth and nineteenth centuries; it is now a museum run by Madame Tussaud's.

WEST WYCOMBE PARK (NT)
West Wycombe, Buckinghamshire HP14 3AJ
Tel: 01494 513569
Eighteenth-century house with an important Rococo landscape garden.

WHITMORE HALL
Whitmore, nr Newcastle-under-Lyme, Staffordshire ST5 5HW
Tel: 01782 680478
Sixteenth-century house extended in the seventeenth century.

WIGHTWICK MANOR (NT)
Wightwick Bank, Wolverhampton, West Midlands WV6 8EE
Tel: 01902 761400
Nineteenth-century house with Morris and Co decoration.

WILTON HOUSE
Wilton, Salisbury, Wiltshire SP2 0BJ.
Tel: 01722 746720 / 01722 746729
Seat of the Earls of Pembroke, Wilton was built in 1543–56 on the site of a medieval Benedictine abbey; it was remodelled in the Palladian style in the 1630s.

WINDSOR CASTLE
Windsor, Berkshire SL4 1NJ
Tel: 02077 667304
The official residence of HM the Queen, originally Norman, the castle was remodelled in the early nineteenth century by Sir Jeffry Wyatville.

WITLEY COURT (EH)
Great Witley, Worcester WR6 6JT
Tel: 01299 896636
Ruin of a large mansion of the seventeenth and eighteenth centuries, Witley originated as an early Jacobean manor house, which was transformed by John Nash in c. 1805 with the addition of huge Ionic porticoes to the north and south fronts. It was remodelled again in the 1850s in the Italianate style by Samuel Daukes.

WOBURN ABBEY
Woburn, Bedfordshire MK17 9WA
Tel: 01525 290666
Seat of the Dukes of Bedford, Woburn originated as a medieval Cistercian monastery. Dissolved in 1543, it was converted to a country house by Sir John Russell in 1619, then rebuilt as a Palladian house by Henry Flitcroft in the 1740s, and further remodelled and extended by Henry Holland in the 1780s.

WOLFETON HOUSE
Dorchester. Dorset DT2 9PN
Tel: 01305 263500
Late fifteenth-century Tudor and Elizabethan courtyard house built in 1480 by Sir John Trenchard, Wolfeton was later remodelled, extended and embellished with plaster ceilings, fireplaces and panelling by Sir George Trenchard in c. 1580, reduced during the eighteenth century.

WOLLATON HALL
Wollaton, Nottingham NG8 2AE
Tel: 01159 153900
An important sixteenth-century house designed by Robert Smythson (now a museum). A classic example of the Elizabethan so-called 'prodigy' house.

GLOSSARY OF TECHNICAL TERMS

ACANTHUS – a stylized ornamental plant motif, resembling an acanthus plant, commonly used in the decoration of CLASSICAL Corinthian COLUMNS, along with other scrolled details (*see also* ORDER, CORINTHIAN).

ACHIEVEMENT – in heraldry, a complete coat of arms.

ARCADE – a series of arches, supported by a series of COLUMNS.

ARCHITRAVE – a moulded frame around a door or window (*see also* MOULDING).

ASHLAR – smooth-faced masonry (typical of GEORGIAN houses).

ATTIC – the upper storey of a house.

BALUSTRADE – a series of short posts supporting a rail.

BASEMENT – the lowest storey of a building.

BAY – the division of a building, both inside and out, into bays: the spaces created by supporting members, such as BAY WINDOWS, wall recesses, COLUMNS, roof-trusses and buttresses (e.g. four windows and a door make a five-bay house).

BAY WINDOW – a window projecting from a FAÇADE (*see also* BAY and ORIEL).

BOLECTION MOULDING – a smooth, curved MOULDING, often joining two elements in panelling.

BOND – the method of laying bricks; with English bond, bricks are laid side-on at one level, and head-on at the next level (the side-face is known as the stretcher, the end-face as the header); with Flemish bond, each layer is made up of alternate headers and stretchers.

BOW WINDOW – a curved projecting window.

CANTILEVER – a horizontal, self-supporting, weight-bearing projection, e.g. a cantilever staircase where the treads are set into the wall.

CAPITAL – the topmost decorative feature of a COLUMN.

CARTOUCHE – a scrolled frame for coats of arms or inscriptions.

CASEMENT – a side-opening window, e.g. opening on a hinge.

CASTELLATED – featuring battlements, or castle-like elements (*see also* CRENELLATION).

CHAIR-RAIL – *see* DADO-RAIL

COLUMN – an upright support, usually rounded and detailed in one of the CLASSICAL ORDERS.

CONSOLE – a decorative scrolled bracket.

CORNICE – the ornamental MOULDING at the top of a wall (or above a COLUMN).

COURSE – a layer or line of bricks or masonry (*see also* BOND).

COVE – a concave MOULDING (especially of a ceiling or cornice).

CRENELLATION – the addition of battlements, giving the outline of a castle (*see also* CASTELLATED).

CROSS-WINDOW – a window with only one MULLION (upright) and one TRANSOM (cross-piece) (typically mid-seventeenth century).

CUPOLA – a small dome, usually crowning a LANTERN or TURRET.

DADO-RAIL/CHAIR-RAIL – a MOULDING at chair height dividing the lower part of an interior wall (the DADO) from the upper part (the infill).

DAIS – a raised floor at the DAIS-END, or high end, of a great hall where the high table stood.

DAIS-END – the upper, or high, end of a great hall or chamber where the high table stood on a raised DAIS.

DENTIL – a small square detail used in a CLASSICAL CORNICE.

DOG-LEG STAIR – a stair where the flights run parallel (i.e. not around an open well).

DOME – a half-spherical roof rising from a circular base (as at St Paul's Cathedral, London).

DORMER – a window that projects out of a sloping roof.

DRESSINGS – the decorative features, added to an ELEVATION, usually made of stone (see also FAÇADE).

EAVES – the part of a roof that projects beyond the supporting wall below.

ELEVATION – the face or FAÇADE of a house.

ENFILADE – a straight alignment of doors to give a long vista (seventeenth-century French).

ENGAGED COLUMN – a column that appears part sunk into a wall (also called attached).

ENTABLATURE – the top part of a CLASSICAL ORDER (divided into ARCHITRAVE, FRIEZE and CORNICE).

EYECATCHER – a building designed to stand out in a view.

FAÇADE – the face of a building as elevation.

FENESTRATION – the style or type of window.

LEFT: *The breathtaking late 18th-century 'imperial'-type staircase designed by James Wyatt at Heaton Hall, Manchester. Note the Corinthian columns on the landing.*

FESTOON – an ornament in the form of a hanging garland.

FINIAL – a decorative detail on the top of a GABLE.

FLUTING – the vertical grooves on a COLUMN.

FRIEZE – the area between the ARCHITRAVE and CORNICE.

GABLE – the triangular end-wall created by a ridge roof.

GIANT ORDER – the use of COLUMNS or PILASTERS that run over two storeys of a building (seventeenth and eighteenth century).

GIBBS SURROUND – a decorative surround to a door or window of exaggerated blocks (associated with the early eighteenth-century architect James Gibbs).

GRISAILLE – decorative painting in a single colour, usually greyish or grey monochrome, sometimes enhanced with gold.

GROTESQUE – an extravagant decorative ornament filled with closely entwined plant, animal or human motifs often in fantastic forms. Painted grotesques were discovered by Renaissance architects on the walls of excavated Roman houses. Named after the underground *grotte* or caves in which they were found, grotesques were popularly used in English architectural decoration from the sixteenth century on.

GROTTO – an artificial cave, decorated with shells, pebbles or rocks (seventeenth, eighteenth and early nineteenth centuries).

HAMMERBEAM ROOF – a form of roof-truss developed in the late fifteenth century in which the arch bearing the roof was supported in large projecting brackets, creating a much more open effect than previously.

HERM – a rectangular pillar, surmounted by a bust or head, originally one portraying the Greek god Hermes (*see also* TERM).

HIPPED ROOF – a roof with GABLES that slope back towards the roof.

HOOD MOULD – a detail designed to throw rainwater off a surface (*see also* MOULDING).

JAMB – the side of an opening, of a door, window or chimneypiece.

KEYSTONE – the wedge-shaped stone in the centre of an arch.

LANCET – a tall, narrow, pointed arch (typically thirteenth century).

LANTERN – a glazed TURRET on a roof, allowing light into the spaces below.

LINENFOLD – a style of decorated panelling with relief carving resembling folded linen cloth (sixteenth century).

LINTEL – a horizontal weight-bearing beam over a door or window.

LOGGIA – an open arcade or series of arches.

MODILLION – the small ornamental bracket (plaster or carved) used in a CORNICE.

MOULDING – a projecting surface (on exteriors usually to project rainwater off the surface).

MULLION – the upright element in a window.

MURAL – a painting done on a wall.

NEWEL – an upright structural member of a staircase.

OGEE – a curved and pointed arch or moulding (fourteenth century).

ORDER(S) – the system of proportion and detail for a CLASSICAL COLUMN (chiefly, Doric, Ionic, Corinthian, also Tuscan and Composite).

ORIEL – a BAY WINDOW for a great hall, or a projecting upper window.

PALMETTE – a stylized CLASSICAL ornamental detail resembling a palm leaf.

PARAPET – a low wall concealing a roof.

PEDIMENT – a low-pitched GABLE above a PORTICO, door or window (usually triangular).

PENDANT – a hanging decorative detail in a plasterwork ceiling, where the ribs cross.

PIANO NOBILE – a principal floor, usually raised over a basement (an Italian concept).

PIER – the solid wall space between windows.

PILASTER – a flat, two-dimensional version of a CLASSICAL COLUMN.

PILE – a term used to describe the depth of a house (one room deep is single-pile, two rooms deep is double-pile).

PLINTH – the base of a COLUMN.

PORTE COCHERE – a porch entrance large enough to allow visitors to dismount in shelter.

PORTICO – a grand porch in CLASSICAL Roman style; a low-pitched roof supported by COLUMNS.

PUTTO (plural *putti*) – a small, naked, chubby, cherubic boy, not necessarily winged (late seventeenth/early eighteenth century).

QUATREFOIL – the four-part shaped head of a GOTHIC window.

QUOIN – a detail emphasizing a house's corner.

RUSTICATION – masonry cut in deep grooves to emphasize solidity, usually on the basement level (eighteenth century).

SCREENS PASSAGE – a passage, created by a screen, running across the kitchen and the entrance end of a great hall; the screen was often highly decorated.

SCROLL – an ornamental detail suggesting a scroll of parchment.

SOFFIT – the visible underside of any projection.

SOLAR – the first floor withdrawing room in a medieval house (also known as the great chamber).

SPANDREL – the area between a MOULDING and an arch.

STRAPWORK – a style of intertwining decoration resembling cut leather.

STRING-COURSE – a continuous MOULDING on the exterior of a building.

STUCCO – a plaster enriched with marble dust (eighteenth century) or external plaster resembling stone (early nineteenth century).

TERM – a tapered pedestal usually crowned by a bust or half-figure (*see also* HERM).

TIMBER-FRAME – the framework of a house, with timbers joined together to create walls (typical of medieval and sixteenth-century architecture).

TRACERY – the decorative divisions of a GOTHIC window.

TRANSOM – the main cross-bar spanning the width, or part width, of a window.

TREFOIL – the three-part (tripartite) leaf-shaped head of a GOTHIC window.

TRIGLYPHS – the three grooves characteristic of the Doric ORDER.

URN – a CLASSICAL vase motif used in decoration.

VENETIAN WINDOW – a three-part window, with a central arched window separated from two narrower openings on either side by COLUMNS (sometimes called Serlian after the Venetian architect Sebastiano Serlio).

VOLUTES – the scrolls that make up the capital of the Ionic ORDER.

WAINSCOT – another word for panelling (particularly in the later seventeenth and early eighteenth centuries).

WEATHERBOARDING – an outer layer of overlapping horizontal boarding on a wall.

LEFT: *The great hall at Ockwells Manor, Berkshire, photographed in 1924 reflects the great passion for collecting armour and old English furniture that developed in the 1890s and early 1900s. Arms had traditionally been hung in great halls so that if the household were under attack there would be a ready supply of arms for immediate defence.*

261

GUIDE TO PERIOD STYLES

The briefest outline of major decorative styles and key periods of architecture is sketched below. To explore period styles more fully, see the bibliography on pages 265–7, or consult Turner, Jane (ed.), *The Dictionary of Art* (Macmillan, 1996).

ART NOUVEAU

(late nineteenth- and early twentieth century)

A turn-of-the-century European decorative style, characterized by exaggerated asymmetry and attenuated, undulating forms, such as writhing plant tendrils, whiplash waves and flowing flames and hair.

ARTS AND CRAFTS MOVEMENT

(late nineteenth and early twentieth century)

Influential movement, associated with William Morris, who looked for originality rather than overt historical imitation, while emphasizing good craftsmanship in building.

BAROQUE

(mid- to late seventeenth century)

A European movement in art and architecture characterized by dramatic movement, exuberant colour, strong contrasts in light and mood and expanded, illusionistic space. The English Baroque in architecture is associated with John Vanbrugh (*see also* RESTORATION).

CAROLINE

(early to mid-seventeenth century)

Architecture and decoration from the reign of Charles I (1625–49), combining traditional TUDOR and ELIZABETHAN trends with the revolutionary CLASSICISM of Inigo Jones (*see also* PALLADIANISM, and *see p. 243* for examples of Caroline houses).

CHINOISERIE

(mid- to late eighteenth century)

Style of interior decoration imitating Chinese and oriental designs, especially associated with European ROCOCO.

CLASSICAL

Generally speaking, the concepts, designs and motifs inspired by the art and architecture of the ancient world (Greece and Rome).

CLASSICISM

(seventeenth, eighteenth and nineteenth centuries)

A style modelled on the qualities traditionally associated with the art and architecture of ancient Greece and Rome, exemplified during the Renaissance by the Italian architect Andrea Palladio (*see also* CLASSICAL, PALLADIANISM and NEO-CLASSICISM).

COMMONWEALTH

(mid-seventeenth century)

Architecture produced during the rule of Oliver Cromwell (1649–59), between the CAROLINE and RESTORATION periods of the Stuarts.

COTTAGE ORNÉ

(late eighteenth to early nineteenth century)

A small, prettified, cottage-like, rustic building inspired by PICTURESQUE aesthetics.

DECORATED GOTHIC

(late thirteenth to mid-fourteenth century)

The second, highly ornamental stage of ENGLISH GOTHIC, identified by arched windows filled with ornate tracery (*see also* EARLY ENGLISH GOTHIC, PERPENDICULAR GOTHIC and PLANTAGENET).

EARLY ENGLISH GOTHIC

(late twelfth to late thirteenth century)

Medieval architecture characterized by small lancet windows, pointed arches and ribbed vaults.

EDWARDIAN

(early twentieth century)

Architecture from the reign of Edward VII (1901–10), characterized by varied cross-currents – GREEK, GOTHIC and TUDOR Revivals, ART NOUVEAU and ARTS AND CRAFTS – and Edwardian BAROQUE, such as the new façade for Buckingham Palace (*see p. 246* for Edwardian houses).

ELIZABETHAN

(mid- to late sixteenth century)

Architecture and decoration from the reign of Elizabeth I (1558–1603), combining traditional GOTHIC and TUDOR influences with contemporary RENAISSANCE, and MANNERISTIC trends, exemplified at Longleat in Wiltshire (*see also* TUDORBETHAN, and *see p. 242* for Elizabethan houses).

ENGLISH GOTHIC

see EARLY ENGLISH GOTHIC, DECORATED GOTHIC, PERPENDICULAR GOTHIC

GEORGIAN

(early eighteenth to early nineteenth century)

A succession of decorative styles associated with the reigns of the 'four Georges': George I, II, III and IV (1714–1830), combining aspects of the RENAISSANCE, ROCOCO, the PICTURESQUE, GOTHIC REVIVAL, PALLADIANISM and NEO-CLASSICISM, but with CLASSICISM predominating in some form (*see pp. 244–5 for Georgian houses; see also* the REGENCY for George IV).

GOTHIC REVIVAL

(mid-eighteenth to mid-nineteenth century)

A revival of medieval GOTHIC forms in both churches and domestic dwellings. From the 1830s the revival was inspired by the designs of A. W. N. Pugin (*see also* EARLY ENGLISH GOTHIC, DECORATED GOTHIC, PERPENDICULAR GOTHIC and ROCOCO GOTHIC).

GREEK REVIVAL

(early nineteenth century)

A solid and sober style of architecture and decoration inspired by the study of ancient Greek architecture.

ITALIANATE STYLE

(nineteenth-century)

Domestic style in the manner of Italian Renaissance villas.

JACOBEAN

(early seventeenth century)

Architectural style associated with the reign of James I (1603–25), more sumptuous than ELIZABETHAN, combining aspects of the RENAISSANCE and MANNERISM, also Dutch curved GABLES and fancy chimneys, pendulous plasterwork and ornate STRAPWORK, grand staircases and MULLIONED windows (*see p. 242 for Jacobean houses*).

LANCASTER AND YORK

The era marked by the upheavals between the royal houses of Lancaster and York, *c.* 1399–1485, coinciding with the beginning of the PERPENDICULAR GOTHIC period of architecture (*see p. 241 for Lancaster and York houses*).

MANNERISM

(mid- to late sixteenth century)

An exaggerated and affected decorative style that developed at the end of the Italian High RENAISSANCE, characterized by a deliberate contradiction of the CLASSSICAL rules for creating harmony, restraint, clarity and order, producing instead fanciful, exaggerated, ornate and unexpected effects (*see also* ELIZABETHAN and JACOBEAN).

MODERNISM

(early twentieth century)

Avant-garde architecture inspired by the International Modern Movement of the 1920s and 1930s, associated with Walter Gropius and Charles-Edouard Le Corbusier, using modern structural technologies, deliberately detached from historical architecture and stripped of arbitrary decoration (*see also* POST-MODERNISM).

NEO-CLASSICAL

(mid-eighteenth century to early nineteenth century)

A revival of CLASSICISM in reaction to the excesses of ROCOCO, but also inspired by contemporary excavations of the ancient Roman cities of Pompeii and Herculaneum, exemplified by the work of Robert Adam and John Nash.

NORMAN STYLE (ROMANESQUE IN EUROPE)

(mid-eleventh to late twelfth century)

The English version of European Romanesque, associated with the Norman Conquest and marked by round-headed openings and massive walls and piers (*see p. 240 for* Norman-style houses).

OLD ENGLISH

(nineteenth century)

Domestic style drawing on the character of medieval and TUDOR farmhouses and manor houses (*see also* VICTORIAN).

PALLADIANISM

(mid-seventeenth and mid-eighteenth centuries)

CLASSICAL (ancient Greco-Roman) architecture mediated through the buildings and books of the sixteenth-century Venetian architect Andrea Palladio, first in the 1620s and 1630s by Inigo Jones, and then in the 1720s and 1730s by Richard Boyle, 3rd Earl of Burlington, William Kent and others.

PERPENDICULAR GOTHIC

(late fourteenth to late fifteenth century)

The final stage of ENGLISH GOTHIC, marked by greater simplicity and angularity, by broad arches, large windows and fan-vaulting, typified at King's College Chapel, Cambridge (*see also* EARLY ENGLISH GOTHIC and DECORATED GOTHIC).

PICTURESQUE, THE

(late eighteenth to early nineteenth century)

Late eighteenth-century term for the aesthetically pleasing irregularity and ruggedness of natural landscapes, exemplified by the paintings of Claude Lorrain. The fashionable appeal of the Picturesque inspired architects to design gardens and buildings 'as if in a picture'.

PLANTAGENET

(mid-twelfth to late fifteenth century)

The era during which the Plantagenet dynasty reigned (1154–1485), spanning late NORMAN, EARLY ENGLISH, DECORATED and PEPENDICULAR GOTHIC styles in architecture (*see p. 240* for Plantagenet houses).

POST-MODERNISM

(mid- to late twentieth-century)

A reaction to MODERNISM in domestic architecture, causing a revival of style, colour and decorative detail.

QUEEN ANNE STYLE

(early eighteenth century)

Architecture and decoration associated with the reign of Queen Anne (1702–14), characterized by Classical simplicity and widespread use of red brick (*see p. 244* for Queen Anne houses).

QUEEN ANNE REVIVAL

(late nineteenth century)

Revival of both QUEEN ANNE and seventeenth-century Dutch styles, influenced by Richard Norman Shaw and characterized by the use of red brick, shaped gables, asymmetry, and diversity of texture.

REGENCY

(early to mid-nineteenth-century)

Decorative and architectural style associated with the Regency of George IV (1810–20), but also encompassing wider stylistic trends from 1800 to 1830, ranging from NEO-CLASSICISM to CHINOISERIE and Egyptian motifs (*see p. 245* for Regency houses).

RENAISSANCE

(mid- to late sixteenth century in Britain)

The cultural revolution, inspired by the rediscovery of CLASSICAL art and literature, which originated in fifteenth-century Italy and spread across Northern Europe during the sixteenth century.

RESTORATION STYLE

(mid- to late seventeenth century)

The art and architecture associated with the Restoration of the Stuarts, Charles II (1660–85) and James I (1685–8), characterized by the opulent English BAROQUE, as well as by oriental lacquer and veneer (*see p. 243* for Restoration houses).

ROCOCO

(mid- to late eighteenth century)

A light, gay decorative style, essentially French, associated with the reign of Louis XV, characterized by soft colours, flowing designs and flowery scrolls, typically charming and elegant in effect.

ROCOCO GOTHIC (GOTHICK)

(mid- to late eighteenth century)

The early phase of the GOTHIC REVIVAL, associated with the pattern books of Batty Langley and Horace Walpole's Strawberry Hill.

SCOTS BARONIAL

(nineteenth-century)

Domestic style popular in VICTORIAN Scotland, recalling medieval and sixteenth-century baronial halls, marked by lively roof lines, bold chimneys, DORMERS and round towers, exemplified by Balmoral Castle in Scotland.

TUDOR

(early to mid-sixteenth century)

Although the Tudor dynasty spanned the reigns of five monarchs (Henry VII, Henry VIII, Mary Tudor, Edward VI and Elizabeth I), in architectural terms Tudor is mainly associated with the reigns of Henry VII and VIII (*see p. 241* for Tudor houses) and PERPENDICULAR GOTHIC.

TUDORBETHAN

(nineteenth-century to early twentieth century)

Domestic architecture taking its style and decorative detail from TUDOR and ELIZABETHAN country houses; also 'Jacobethan' for mixture of JACOBEAN and ELIZABETHAN.

VICTORIAN

(mid- to end nineteenth century)

Architecture from the reign of Queen Victoria (1837–1901), combining a wide variety of styles and revivals, ranging from ITALIANATE to GOTHIC REVIVAL, OLD ENGLISH and SCOTS BARONIAL, but marked by a new use of materials, such as glass and cast iron, and new building types, such as the suburban villa (*see p. 246* for Victorian houses).

SOURCES AND SELECTED FURTHER READING

For a general overview of English architecture, I always recommend the brilliant cartoonist and humorist Lancaster, Osbert, *Homes, Sweet Homes* (John Murray, 1939), a mild parody of 1000 years of English domestic architecture, with amusing cartoons, but still a worthy introduction. Also, Girouard, Mark, *Life in the English Country House: A Social and Architectural History* (Yale University Press, 1978), is one of the most illuminating books on the English country house.

For county guides, an invaluable series is Pevsner, Nikolaus *et al.* (eds.), *The Buildings of England* (Penguin Books, 1951–, Yale University Press, 2002–), which, along with its sister series on Scotland, Wales and Ireland (the latter in progress), has been constantly updated and extended. For a wide range of subjects on art and architecture, Turner, Jane (ed.), *The Dictionary of Art* (Macmillan, 1996) is indispensable.

COUNTRY HOUSES AND ENGLISH ARCHITECTURE

Aslet, Clive and Powers, Alan, *The National Trust Book of the English House* (Penguin: Harmondsworth, in association with The National Trust, 1985).

Beard, Geoffrey *The National Trust Book of the English House Interior* (Penguin: Harmondsworth, in association with The National Trust, 1991).

Brunskill, R. W., *Brick Building in Britain* (Gollancz in association with Peter Crawley, 1990, 1997).

Calloway, Stephen (ed.), *The Elements of Style: An Encyclopedia of Domestic Architectural Detail* (Mitchell Beazley, 1996, 2004).

Chambers, James, *The English House* (Thames Methuen, 1985).

Fleming, John, Honour, Hugh and Pevsner, Nikolaus (eds.), *The Penguin Dictionary of Architecture* (Penguin: Harmondsworth, 1980).

Girouard, Mark, *A Country House Companion* (Century, 1987).

Gray, Edmund, *The British House: A Concise Architectural History* (Barrie & Jenkins, 1994).

Hall, Michael, *The English Country House: From the Archives of Country Life 1897–1939* (Mitchell Beazley, 1994).

Harris, John, *The Artist and the Country House: A History of Country House and Garden View Painting in Britain, 1540–1870* (Philip Wilson for Sotheby Parke Bernet, 1979).

Harris, John, *No Voice from the Hall: Early Memories of a Country House Snooper* (John Murray, 2000).

Jackson, Anna, *The V&A Guide to Period Styles: 400 Years of British Art and Design* (V&A Publications, 2002).

Lees-Milne, James (ed.), *The Country House* (Oxford University Press, 1982).

Lees-Milne, James, *Diaries, 1942–1945: Ancestral Voices and Prophesying Peace* (John Murray, 1995).

Lever, Jill and Harris, John, *Illustrated Dictionary of Architecture, 800–1914* (Faber and Faber, 1993).

Lloyd, Nathaniel, *A History of the English House from Primitive Times to the Victorian Period* (Architectural Press, 1931).

Mandler, Peter, *The Fall and Rise of the Stately Home* (Yale University Press, 1997).

Montgomery-Massingberd, Hugh, *Great Houses of England and Wales* (Laurence King, 2000)..

Montgomery-Massingberd, Hugh, *English Manor Houses* (Laurence King, 2001).

Musson, Jeremy, *The English Manor House: From the Archives of Country Life* (Aurum, 1999).

Osborne, A. L., *The Country Life Pocket Guide to English Domestic Architecture* (Country Life, 1967).

Watkin, David, *English Architecture: A Concise History* (Thames & Hudson, 2001).

Willes, Margaret, *Historic Interiors: A Photographic Tour* (The National Trust, 1999).

Wilson, Richard and Mackley, Alan, *Creating Paradise: the Building of the English Country House, 1660–1880* (Hambledon and London, 2000).

Worsley, Giles, *England's Lost Houses: From the Archives of Country Life* (Aurum, 2002).

NORMAN TO MEDIEVAL

Brown, R. J., *Timber-Framed Buildings of England* (Robert Hale, 1997).

Fernie, Eric, *The Architecture of Norman England* (Oxford University Press, 2000).

Marks, Richard and Williamson, Paul (eds.), assisted by Townsend, Eleanor, *Gothic: Art for England 1400–1547*, exhibition catalogue (V&A Publications, 2003).

Wood, Margaret, *The English Mediaeval House* (Phoenix House, 1965, Studio Editions, 1994).

TUDOR TO STUART

Airs, Malcom, *The Tudor & Jacobean Country House: A Building History* (Alan Sutton, 1995).

Cooper, Nicholas, *Houses of the Gentry, 1480–1680* (Yale University Press in association with English Heritage, 1999).

Girouard, Mark, *Robert Smythson and the Elizabethan Country House* (Yale University Press, 1983, 1985).

Hill, Oliver and Cornforth, John, *English Country Houses: Caroline, 1625–1685* (Country Life Books, 1966).

Lees-Milne, James, *English Country Houses. Baroque, 1685–1715* (Country Life Books, 1970).

Mowl, Tim, *Elizabethan & Jacobean Style* (Phaidon Press, 1993).

Platt, Colin, *The Great Rebuildings of Tudor and Stuart England: Revolutions in Architectural Taste* (UCL Press, 1994).

Thurley, Simon, *The Royal Palaces of Tudor England: Architecture and Court Life, 1460–1547* (Yale University Press, 1993).

GEORGIAN TO REGENCY

Christie, Christopher, *The British Country House in the Eighteenth Century* (Manchester University Press, 2000).

Cornforth, John, *English Interiors 1790–1848: The Quest for Comfort* (Barnes and Jenkins, 1978).

Cornforth, John, *Early Georgian Interiors* (Yale University Press, 2004).

Cruickshank, Dan, *A Guide to the Georgian Buildings of Britain and Ireland* (Weidenfeld & Nicolson, 1985).

Curl, James Stevens, *Georgian Architecture* (David & Charles, 1993).

Hussey, Christopher, *English Country Houses: Mid Georgian, 1760–1800* (Country Life Books, 1956).

Hussey, Christopher, *English Country Houses: Late Georgian 1800–1840* (Country Life Books, 1958).

Hussey, Christopher, *English Country Houses: Early Georgian, 1715–1760* (Country Life Books, 1965).

Parissien, Steven, *Adam Style* (Phaidon Press, 1992).

Robinson, John Martin, *The Regency Country House: From the Archives of Country Life* (Aurum Press, 2005).

Worsley, Giles, *Classical Architecture in Britain: The Heroic Age* (Yale University Press, 1994).

VICTORIAN

Dixon, Roger and Muthesius, Stefan, *Victorian Architecture* (Thames & Hudson, 1978).

Franklin, Jill, *The Gentleman's Country House and Its Plan, 1835–1914* (Routledge & Kegan Paul, 1981).

Girouard, Mark, *The Victorian Country House* (Yale University Press, 1979).

Orbach, Julian, *Blue Guide: Victorian Architecture in Britain* (W. W. Norton & Co., 1987).

Saint, Andrew, *Richard Norman Shaw* (Yale University Press for the Paul Mellon Centre for Studies in British Art, 1976).

TWENTIETH CENTURY

Aslet, Clive, *The Last Country Houses* (Yale University Press, 1982).

Gradidge, Roderick, *Dream Houses: The Edwardian Ideal* (Constable, 1980).

Gray, A. Stuart, *Edwardian Architecture: A Biographical Dictionary* (Duckworth, 1985).

Muthesius, Herman, *The English House 1904–05*, translated by Janet Seligman (Crosby Lockwood Staples, 1979).

Powers, Alan, *Twentieth Century Houses: From the Archives of Country Life* (Aurum Press, 2004).

Robinson, John Martin, *The Latest Country Houses* (Bodley Head, 1984).

Stamp, Gavin, *Edwin Lutyens: Country Houses: From the Archives of Country Life* (Aurum Press, 2001).

COUNTRY HOUSE ARCHITECTS

Colvin, Howard, *A Biographical Dictionary of British Architects, 1600–1840* (Yale University Press for the Paul Mellon Centre for Studies in British Art, 1995),

Goldman, Lawrence (ed.), *Dictionary of National Biography* (Oxford University Press, 2004–), also known as the ODNB.

COUNTRY HOUSE GARDENS

Dixon Hunt, John and Willis, Peter (eds.), *The Genius of the Place: The English Landscape Garden 1620–1820* (MIT Press, 1988).

Elliott, Brent, *The Country House Garden: From the Archives of Country Life, 1897–1939* (Mitchell Beazley, 1995).

Goode, Patrick and Lancaster, Michael (eds.), *The Oxford Companion to Gardens* (Oxford University Press, 1987).

Phaidon, *The Garden Book* (Phaidon Press, 2003).

Taylor, Patrick, *The Gardens of Britain & Ireland* (Dorling Kindersley, 2003, 2004).

LANDOWNING FAMILIES

Burke, J. B., Burke's *Genealogical and Heraldic History of the Landed Gentry*, or *Burke's Landed Gentry* for short (Burke's Peerage Ltd, 1972).

Kidd, Charles *et al.* (eds.), *Debrett's Peerage and Baronetage* (Macmillan, 2002–).

SERVANTS, KITCHENS AND STABLES

Horn, Pamela, *The Rise and Fall of the Victorian Servant* (Alan Sutton, 1990, 1995).

Horn, Pamela, *Flunkeys and Scullions: Life Below Stairs in Georgian England* (Sutton Publishing, 2004).

Sambrook, Pamela A. and Brears, Peter (eds.), *The Country House Kitchen, 1650–1900* (Sutton Publishing, 1996).

Waterfield, Giles, French, Anne and Craske, Matthew, *Below Stairs: 40 Years of Servants' Portraits*, exhibition catalogue (National Portrait Gallery Publications, 2003).

Waterson, Merlin, *The Servants' Hall: A Domestic History of Erddig* (Routledge and Kegan Paul, 1980, republished 1990).

Worsley, Giles, *The British Stable* (Yale University Press, 2004).

SYMBOLS AND CONTENTS

Brooke-Little, J. P. (ed.), *Boutell's Heraldry: Revised by J. P. Brooke-Little* (Frederick Warne & Co. Ltd., 1973, 1978).

Clarke, G. B., (ed.), *Descriptions of Lord Cobham's Gardens at Stowe (1700–1750)* (Buckinghamshire Record Society, 1990).

Fleming, John and Honour, Hugh, *The Penguin Dictionary of Decorative Arts* (Allen Lane, 1977, Viking, 1989).

Gaunt, Willam, *Court Painting in England from Tudor to Victorian Times* (Constable, 1980).

Glanville, Philippa (ed.), *Silver* (V&A Publications, 1996).

Hall, James, *Dictionary of Subjects and Symbols in Art* (John Murray, 1984).

Jackson-Stops, Gervase, *et al.* (eds.), *The Fashioning and Functioning of the British Country House*, exhibition catalogue (Washington DC National Gallery of Art, 1989).

Jackson-Stops, Gervase (ed.), *The Treasure Houses of Britain: Five Hundred Years of Private Patronage and Art Collecting* (Yale University Press, 1985).

Lodwick, Marcus, *The Gallery Companion: Understanding Western Art* (Thames & Hudson 2002).

Potter, Alexander and Margaret, *Interiors* (John Murray, 1957).

Waterfield, Giles, Hearn, Karen and Upstone, Robert (eds.), *In Celebration: The Art of the Country House*, exhibition catalogue (Tate Gallery Publications, 1998).

Waterhouse, Ellis, *Painting in Britain 1530 to 1790* (Pelican History of Art, Penguin: Harmondsworth, 1978).

Wells-Cole, Anthony, *Art and Decoration in Elizabethan and Jacobean England: The Influence of Continental Prints 1558–1625* (Yale University Press, 1997).

Wilton, Andrew and Bignamini, Ilaria (eds.), *The Grand Tour: the Lure of Italy in the Eighteenth Century*, exhibition catalogue (Tate Gallery Publications, 1996).

Woodcock, Thomas, and Robinson, John Martin, *Heraldry in National Trust Houses* (The National Trust, 1999).

VISITORS' HANDBOOKS

English Heritage, *English Heritage Members and Visitors Handbook* (English Heritage, 2004, published annually).

Godfrey-Fausset, Charlie, *Footprint England Handbook* (Footprint Handbooks, 2003).

Greeves, Lydia and Trinick, Michael, *The National Trust Guide* (The National Trust, 1989).

Hudson, Norman, *Hudson's Historic Houses & Gardens* (N. Hudson, 2004, published annually).

Jenkins, Simon, *England's Thousand Best Houses* (Allen Lane, 2003).

National Trust (Great Britain), *The National Trust Handbook for Members and Visitors* (The National Trust, 2004, published annually).

Tyack, Geoffrey, and Brindle, Stephen, *Blue Guide: Country Houses of England* (W. W. Norton & Co., 1994).

ACKNOWLEDGEMENTS

In writing any book of this kind, one is inevitably indebted to many other authors – who are cited in the adjoining reading list –and I would be particularly like to mention Mark Girouard, Geoffrey Beard, John Cornforth, David Watkin and Simon Jenkins. I am immensely grateful to the Ebury Press team for their encouragement and industry, Carey Smith, Sarah Lavelle and Belinda Wilkinson, and David Fordham for his inspired design. Also special thanks to the *Country Life* Picture Library team, Camilla Costello, Paula Fahey, Lara Platman, Leonora Trafford, Leora Morrell and Eleanor Sier, for all their patient support with my picture selection and the processing of the wonderful images in which their library is so rich.

Many thanks also to my *Country Life* colleagues, especially Caroline Scott, Clive Aslet and Fiona Dent. Many friends have been generous with their time to discuss particular themes, especially, Michael Hall, John Hardy, John Goodall, Mary Miers, Tim Richardson, Kathryn Bradley-Hole, Houn Mallalieu, Peter Clark, John Martin Robinson, Wil Palin and John Maddison. Any errors are, of course, my own.

I would particularly like to thank the owners, curators, supporting staff and volunteers at all the country houses featured and of all the hundreds of houses I have enjoyed visiting for *Country Life* over the past decade, for their generosity in opening and sharing these houses with a wider public.

Above all, I want to thank my wife, Sophie, and our children, Georgia and Miranda, for their support, patience and love, and for giving me the time to pen these words.

All of the photographs in this book are from the *Country Life* Picture Archive. The publishers thank the archive and the following individual photographers for the use of their work:

Paul Barker 2, 6, 10, 18, 33, 34, 43, 67, 81, 90, 103, 121, 131, 133, 134, 135, 154, 155, 162, 163, 173, 195, 201, 202, 223, 229, 233, 238, 239; Clive Boursnell 75, 220, 227, 237; June Buck 39, 42, 66, 119, 126, 131, 145, 167, 218, 234, 247; Mark Fiennes 55, 70, 127; Jonathan Gibson 25, 88, 123, 148, 243(iii), 246(ii); Arthur Gill 102, 141l; 151, 165, 196, 240(i); A. E. Henson 13l, 29, 45, 46, 53, 56, 60r, 76, 92, 96, 107, 109b, 111, 141r, 158, 197, 212, 261, 240(ii), 241(i), 242(i), 244(i), 244(iii); Keith Hewitt 3; Anne Hyde 221, 230; Tim Imrie-Tait 9, 13r, 19, 30, 40, 62, 87, 91, 99, 101t, 114, 117, 122, 128, 137, 149, 159, 169, 170, 176, 198, 255, 258; Craig Knowles 95; Brian Moody 183; Julian Nieman 7, 15, 24, 26, 83, 109t, 115, 147; Alex Ramsay 23, 78, 181, 191, 199, 207, 240(iii); Alex Starkey 37, 65, 73, 97, 118, 125, 129, 132, 138, 180, 184, 192, 245(i), 243(iii), 246(i); Simon Upton 174, 216; F. W. Westley 36, 93, 142, 244(ii), 268.

LEFT: *Typical of late 16th-century panelling, the wainscot at Burton Agnes Hall, Yorkshire, incorporates a series of miniature arches set within the panels, as well as room-height pilasters dividing the interior visually into bays. Both elements of Classical detailing had, by this time, been absorbed into English country house architecture.*

Index

INDEX